The Great Irish Famine

The Great Irish Famine

Prepared for The Economic History Society by

Cormac Ó Gráda

Statutory Lecturer in Economics
University College
Dublin

GILL & MACMILLAN

Published by the Press Syndicate of the University of Cambridge
The Pitt Building, Trumpington Street, Cambridge CB2 1RP
40 West 20th Street, New York, NY 10011-4211, USA
10 Stamford Road, Oakleigh, Melbourne 3166, Australia

Printed in Great Britain at the University Press, Cambridge

A catalogue record for this book is available from the British Library

Library of Congress cataloguing in publication data

Ó Gráda, Cormac.
  The great Irish famine/prepared for the Econoic History Society by
Cormac Ó Gráda.
      p.   cm. – (New studies in economic and social history)
    Includes bibliographical references and index.
    ISBN 0 521 55266 4. – ISBN 0 521 55787 9 (pbk.)
    1. Famines – Ireland – History – 19th century. 2. Ireland – History –
1837–1901. I. Title. II. Series.
DA950.7.037   1995
941.508–dc20   95–10860
                                                                          CIP

ISBN 0 521 55266 4 hardback
ISBN 0 521 55787 9 paperback

Contents

Preface

The Great Irish Famine is a 'big' topic, a landmark in Irish and world history. Its causes are controversial, its consequences important wherever the ensuing Irish diaspora reached. The relevant literature is very large. And so my efforts at keeping the bibliography within bounds made the number of footnotes grow and grow. In addition, the Famine is a multidisciplinary subject, featuring research by economists, political scientists, demographers, and historians of diet and agriculture. I have tried to keep the amount of specialist jargon to a minimum, but some inevitably has crept in. In order to keep the account accessible, but without losing all the subtlety of specialized work, I have added a short glossary of technical terms.

I would like to thank the following for reading earlier drafts of this work, and for their criticisms and advice: Michael Anderson, Frank Barry, Leslie Clarkson, Louis Cullen, Fergus D'Arcy, David Dickson, David Fitzpatrick, Liam Kennedy, Michael Laffan, Joel Mokyr, Peter Solar, Brendan Walsh, Ron Weir, and Tony Wrigley. Remaining mistakes are mine alone.

St Patrick's Day 1988
Dublin   CORMAC Ó GRÁDA

Introduction

History provides many examples of famines that cost more human lives than the Great Irish Famine. Reliable evidence on famine casualties tends to be skimpy, but fine comparisons are not called for: enough to note that in northern China in 1877–8 a famine accounted for 9 to 13 million deaths, and in 1932–3 in the Ukraine another for probably at least 3 million; or that, by a recent reckoning, the dreadful Bengali famine of 1940–3 carried off 10 millions. In this league of doom the cost of Ireland's misfortune – about one million lives – may seem small. Measured in proportionate terms, however, the Irish famine's toll exceeded these others, though even in Ireland itself, a lesser-known famine in 1740–1 may have killed a higher share of the people. Still, the 'Great Hunger' has gained wider and more lasting notoriety than most famines. There are several reasons for this. The first is its popularity as a case study in Malthusian exegesis. The price paid by the reckless Irish for their high nuptiality and their large families – both widely noted at the time – is often singled out as a particularly stark instance of the 'principle of population' in action. Second, to students of economics everywhere the Famine recalls an example, however dubious, of that elusive phenomenon, the 'Giffen' good (*).[1] The Irish poor, so it was claimed, in desperation flouted the law of demand by demanding more potatoes as their price rose. Third, to proponents of an old-time, nationalist version of Irish history, the Famine is central. It is the historical wrong that sealed the fate of the unhappy Union between Britain

---

[1]   Terms marked with a star are explained in the glossary.

1

and Ireland: a partner so uncaring in time of need deserved no loyalty from Irishmen.

Yet another reason for the Famine's notoriety is its lateness and context. Famine had effectively disappeared from England by 1600 and from most of Scotland by 1700. Elsewhere in western Europe, the *crises de subsistence* of the eighteenth century were minor affairs by comparison. Far worse, at least in relative terms, than the misnamed 'last great subsistence crisis of the western world' – the famine affecting much of Europe in 1816–19 – the Great Irish Famine struck in what was, after all, the back garden of 'the workshop of the world'. While plans for a 'Great Exhibition' were being hatched in London, thousands were still dying of famine diseases in Ireland. Yet Ireland had been a fully fledged member of the United Kingdom since 1801. The Famine is thus a reminder of how unevenly the benefits of the Industrial Revolution had diffused by the 1840s. Finally, most famines in history have been the product of either bad weather or the effects of war and politics. But the Irish famine had an unusual origin: it was set off by an ecological disaster. For all these reasons, Ireland's Great Famine is familiar.

Curiously, the tragedy has attracted little serious academic research. In Ireland itself the neglect is striking. The professional journals there rarely feature the Famine, and the fullest narrative account of it is by a non-specialist, Cecil Woodham-Smith, who was drawn to the topic by her interest in the third Earl of Lucan (of Crimean War fame). Here is an instance, then, where Clio's Irish devotees have by and large heeded the maxim that 'Anglo-Irish history is for Englishmen to remember, for Irishmen to forget'.[2] But if Irish historians have focused their researches on other, often less controversial matters, a populist and sometimes facile understanding of the tragedy still permeates Irish folk memory. Half-truths about shiploads of grain leaving the country, about a callous and indolent landlordism, and about Queen Victoria subscribing a £5 note to Famine relief are common currency: so are true tales of famine graves and mass evictions. For Ireland today these stories are the Famine's most enduring legacy. Perhaps because such stories are prone to take on a nationalist twist, scholarly Irish

[2]   H. Plunkett (1904) *Ireland in the New Century* (Dublin), p. 26.

assessments of the Famine years tend to be detached and clinical; indeed, their 'generosity and restraint' have been applauded by Woodham-Smith (Woodham-Smith, 1962, *75–6*), and debunking the populist version of folklorists and novelists is their driving theme. Ironically Woodham-Smith's own much-read account, which dwelt on horrific depictions of the crisis and on administrative culpability and ineptitude, was poorly received – or, worse, ignored – by Irish academic historians for being too 'emotive' and 'simplistic'. The condescending review in *Irish Historical Studies*[3] was typical, but perhaps the essay topic set for University College Dublin history students in one of their final exams in 1963 – '*The Great Hunger* is a great novel' – best captures the tone of indignant ridicule that greeted it. The gap between popular perception and classroom orthodoxy has endured: in a 1986 survey poor Woodham-Smith is dismissed in one withering footnote (Daly, 1986, *136*).

When the mysterious fungus *Phytophthora infestans* reached Ireland in August 1845 the potato, which produced the nutritional value of corn at about one-third the cost, was the main food of well over half its people. This left the poor, whose income was largely determined by the cost of growing potatoes, no prospect of trading down to a cheaper food. Bad harvests three years in succession thus posed an unprecedented challenge for relief agencies, and arguably made disaster inevitable. To that extent the story of the Famine is simple. But why the potato's fatal fascination for the Irish? It was, so it is alleged, always a risky proposition: a fickle plant, its bulk and perishability compounded its dangers. Still the Irish poor – and through them the farmers and landlords who employed them – came to depend on it more and more over time, and even substituted high-yielding but unreliable for allegedly safer varieties. Hence the claim that the crisis of 1845–9 had its roots deep in Irish history. A second major theme concerns the efficacy of action taken. Here opinion ranges from that caught in fiery nationalist John Mitchel's accusation that 'the Almighty sent the potato blight, but the English created the Famine' (in Miller, 1985, *306*) to William Wilde's claim that 'the most strenuous efforts which human sagacity, ingenuity and foresight could at the time

---

[3]   By F. S. L. Lyons (1964–5) 14, 76–9.

devise were put into requisition'.[4] While no academic historian takes seriously any more the claim of 'genocide', the issue of blame remains controversial. Many historians shy away from it, though recent scholarship (mainly the work of non-Irish historians) has been facing the issue again. A full appraisal calls for an analysis of the pre-famine economy, so first a brief review of recent work in the area is provided. This is followed by an account of the Famine itself and, finally, an assessment of the impact of the crisis on Irish economy and society.

[4]   *The Census of Ireland for the Year 1851*, Part 5, *Tables of Death*, vol. I, *Containing the Report, Tables of pestilences, and Analysis of the Tables of Death* (2087-I) H.C. 1856, XXIX, 261.

1

Population and potatoes: the pre-Famine context

In most accounts of pre-Famine economic history the key feature is population. Cross-country comparisons of growth rates show why. Taking the period covered in Kenneth Connell's classic *The Population of Ireland 1750–1845* (Connell, 1950) as a unit, among European countries only Finland, Hungary and England seem to have rivalled Ireland's population growth (Table 1.1). Accurate pre-censal estimates of Irish population are impossible, but Connell himself probably underestimated that growth, and recent estimates based on a reworking of the standard sources suggest that numbers trebled in the pre-famine century (Daultrey, Dickson and Ó Gráda, 1981). Such headlong population growth helps explain stories of a country, lemming-like, on the road to disaster.

(i) Demographic trends

By the 1820s and 1830s the effects of the extra numbers were there for all to see. Again and again, travellers noted them in the endemic begging and in the ramshackle cabins and ragged clothes of an underemployed peasantry. Off the beaten track, the margin of cultivation reached bogs and dizzy slopes never cultivated before or since. International comparisons of land/labour ratios might be expected to highlight Ireland's plight. In practice they are less telling, because of differences in the quality of land. Still, in Ireland in 1845 the population density of arable land was about 700 per square mile, and the agricultural population per tilled acre was probably the highest in Europe. To unsentimental observers such as English economist Nassau Senior, the appropriate analogy was a

Table 1.1 *Some comparative population growth rates, 1700–1845 (percentages per annum)*

1700–1845		1750–1845	
France	0.4	France	0.4
England	0.8	England	1.0
Ireland	0.8	Ireland	1.3
		Scotland	0.8
		Sweden	0.7
		Finland	1.0
		Denmark (1769–1845)	0.7

Sources: (Mokyr and Ó Gráda, 1984) and B. R. Mitchell (1975), *European Historical Statistics* (London), pp. 19–25.

'rabbit warren'. Yet the verdict of modern research is that Irish population growth was slackening long before the Famine. Recent revisions of tax-based and censal data imply that population growth in Ireland fell from 1.6 per cent in 1780–1821 to 0.9 per cent in the 1820s, and had dropped as low as 0.6 per cent in 1830–45 (Daultrey, Dickson and Ó Gráda, 1981; Lee, 1981). That last figure is modest by European standards of the day.

National averages mask considerable regional variation. In most areas badly hit by the Famine, population growth was still very rapid in the 1820s and 1830s. Yet even there growth was slowing down. In the five counties (out of a total of thirty-two) growing fastest in 1791–1821, the rate fell from 2.1 per cent then to 1.4 per cent in 1821–41. That such adjustment took place even in the poorest and remotest counties is an important, often neglected point. Instantaneous adjustment is not to be expected: on the contrary, some 'overshooting' due to previous growth and momentum was inevitable. Meanwhile in the midlands and in south- and mid-Ulster population growth on the eve of the Famine was very modest indeed. On these numbers at least, the story that before the Famine Ireland was not facing up to its demographic problems is a myth.

Ireland's odd, sometimes grotesque, population history has long been the stuff of Irish economic-historical debate (Mokyr and Ó Gráda, 1984). The role of nuptiality and fertility, stressed in Connell's classic monograph (Connell, 1950), finds little support elsewhere in contemporary Europe, though it is highlighted by Wrigley and Schofield in their recent account of the English experience. In England the case is based on the sophisticated manipulation of parish register data. In Ireland it must rest instead on largely impressionistic evidence. Admittedly there is a lot of this, a consistent thread through the centuries. In the early seventeenth century it was already being said of Irishwomen that 'their propensity to generation causeth that they cannot endure. They are women at thirteen, and olde wives at thirty'.[5] The same claim is echoed later by many others (Connell, 1950, *46–59*). In the mid-1830s the Irish Poor Inquiry presented plentiful though unsystematic evidence for early marriage. But the firmest pre-Famine quantitative evidence, that provided by the 1841 census, suggests that on the eve of the Famine the average age at marriage (AAM) in Ireland was not exceptionally low (Drake, 1963). Indeed Hajnal's 'singulate mean age' at marriage – roughly the average age at which those who married between the ages of 15 and 50 were married – was over 30 for men born around 1820, and 26 for women.[6] Malthus would (or should) have been impressed by such 'moral restraint'. Alternatively, inferring the median marriage age from the marriage tables in the 1841 census suggests figures of 27.5 years for men and 23.6 years for women. Since typically the age distribution of marriage is skewed (*) to the right – so that the mean is greater than the median – these two sets of numbers are quite compatible. There was fair regional variation in AAM on the eve of the Famine; by Hajnal's measure women's AAM ranged from 25.0 years in Connacht to 26.8 in Leinster, enough to add an extra child to the average family in Connacht. Cottage industry boosted nuptiality (Almquist, 1979). There were class contrasts too. In the county Cavan parish of Killashandra, before the Famine the mean marriage age of farmers' sons was four years higher than that of labourers (K. O'Neill, 1984, *178*).

There can be no doubt about emigration as a factor in depressing the rate of population growth, however. Between Waterloo and the Famine over 1.5 million people left Ireland for good, and the

5   C. L. Faulkner (1904) *Illustrations of Irish History and Topography* (London), p. 357.
6   D. Fitzpatrick (1985) 'Marriage in Post-Famine Ireland', in A. Cosgrove (ed.), *Marriage in Ireland* (Dublin), p. 130.

annual rate was increasing over time, though prone to large fluctuations. This outflow was truly massive for its day: between 1815 and 1845 Ireland provided one-third of all voluntary trans-Atlantic movement. Though dwarfed by later flows, the pre-Famine exodus seems to have accounted for as much as one-sixth or one-seventh of all voluntary trans-Atlantic migration between the time of Columbus and the first steamships.[7] Across Irish regions, pre-Famine emigration was uneven; age-cohort depletion (*) indicates that it was proportionately greatest from north Leinster and south and west Ulster, and lowest from the poorer counties of the south and west (Fitzpatrick, 1984). Did a 'poverty trap' (*) reduce the emigration rate? That many of those cottiers and labourers who lacked the money to buy food during the Famine also lacked the funds to emigrate before 1845 would seem a safe bet. The full cost of a labourer's passage to North America – not just the fare but his subsistence for a few months – was equivalent to perhaps one year's wages. Moving large cottier families was usually out of the question, because credit was rarely forthcoming, and aid was rare. State- and landlord-assisted emigration accounted for no more than a tiny fraction, three or four per cent, of those who left between Waterloo and the Famine (Fitzpatrick, 1984, *14–21*). Colonization schemes were difficult to organize, but even a free passage for another ten or fifteen thousand a year after 1815 would have reduced pressure on the land.

When quizzed by officialdom, the poor professed an eagerness to go, if subsidized. Still, migration to Britain was not costly, and the earnings gap between Britain and Ireland on the eve of the Famine was significant. Why did not more go? Hardly out of ignorance, for thousands from the remote west made the journey there as harvest migrants each year, while thousands more migrated within Ireland. Before 1845, though, this seasonal movement tended to replace a more permanent emigration. Like the potato and cottage industry, it accommodated population pressure on the land. Indeed the apparent rise in the seasonal outflow in the 1820s and 1830s may be linked to the decline of textile production in the west. Thus before the Famine the low rate of permanent

---

[7]   Compare the numbers given in C. McAvedy and R. Jones (1978) *Atlas of World Population History* (Harmondsworth), pp. 30–1.

emigration from the poorer areas had both a cultural and financial basis.

Given its regional mix and the relative wealth and youth of those who left, did emigration deprive the country of a disproportionate share of its human capital? The adverse economic consequences of a 'drain' of brains and skills have been documented (Mokyr, 1980b), but together they do not erase the benefit of emigration to those who really counted, the poor who stayed behind. Emigration reduced land pressure, and in its absence average incomes would have fallen further. Yet migration fits uncomfortably in the positive-versus-preventive check schema suggested by Thomas Malthus in 1798. On the one hand, by reducing numbers emigration averted deaths, on the other, it did so least where it was needed most, and it may also have allowed the maintenance of a high birth rate. Emigration's role may thus seem somewhat contradictory. If it increased inter-regional income disparities within Ireland before 1845, it also reduced the gap between Ireland and outside. This safety-valve aspect grew with time as the outflow became more proletarian.

Combining quantitative and qualitative evidence suggests that both the early growth of population and the pre-Famine adjustment were also linked to AAM. There are some statistical straws in the wind before 1845; local evidence points to some rise in AAM in Dublin and in Cavan in the 1820s and 1830s, but no change in Antrim, while an aggregate exercise based on censal data indicates a drop in the birth rate between 1821 and 1841 (K. O'Neill, 1984; Boyle and Ó Gráda, 1986, 64). Certainly the AAM implied by the 1841 census is high enough to have allowed an earlier rise in AAM some role in the adjustment. Moreover, it is hard to discount all the evidence, admittedly qualitative, in favour of a low Irish AAM in the eighteenth century and earlier; the crux is the timing of the increase in the marriage age. The marriage tables in the 1841 census show evidence of only a feeble rise in the 1830s, suggesting that most of the adjustment in AAM had occurred earlier. The proportions who never married probably rose too before the Famine. Here the comparison between Thomas Newenham's reference in 1805 to the 'extraordinary frequency of marriage among the people of Ireland, which has so often been remarked by strangers',[8] and the high proportion of never-marrieds indicated by the 1841 census – one-eighth of women aged 45–54 years – is tantalizing.

Did mortality contribute to population trends? There is a strong Malthusian presumption for a rise in the death rate, at least after 1800, but evidence is elusive. To complicate matters, the number of famine deaths (see below) was probably falling, and the incidence of one major killer disease, smallpox, was declining too. Indeed Razzell[8a] has claimed for smallpox inoculation the main credit for raising Irish population growth after 1770 or so. Neither smallpox's power to destroy before then nor the chronology of the diffusion of inoculation thereafter are known. True, the available data for Dublin city are impressive enough: smallpox accounted for one-fifth of all reported deaths there in 1661–1745, but for only one in thirty in the 1830s. Dublin's experience was not repeated around the country, though. Just before the Famine smallpox was responsible for only 7 per cent of deaths of Dublin children aged 5 years and under, compared with 11 per cent nationally and 16 per cent in Limerick City. Thus though inoculation reduced mortality, its role was not central. Indeed there was a *positive* association across counties on the eve of the Famine between the risk of dying from smallpox and population growth. In sum, the evidence for a reduction in life expectancy before the Great Famine – if such there was – is not yet to hand.

The outcome suggests that something like the eclectic model of population growth proposed by Ronald Lee for eighteenth-century England[9] also fits Ireland to 1815 or so. Its starting point is straight from Malthus. The birth rate is taken to be an increasing, and the death rate a decreasing function of the prevailing real wage level; population growth, in other words, rises with wages. The demand for labour (and hence population) is governed by the Law of Diminishing Returns. There is an equilibrium wage that generates

---

[8]   *A Statistical and Historical Inquiry into the Magnitude and Progress of the Population of Ireland* (London, 1805), p. 18.

[8a] P. E. Razzell (1970) 'Population growth and economic change in eighteenth and early nineteenth century England and Ireland', in E. L. Jones and G. E. Mingay (eds), *Land, Labour and Population in the Industrial Revolution* (London), pp. 260–81.

[9]   E.g. R. D. Lee (1980) 'A Historical Perspective on Economic Aspects of the Population Explosion: The Case of Preindustrial England', in R. A. Easterlin (ed.), *Population and Economic Change in Developing Countries* (Chicago).

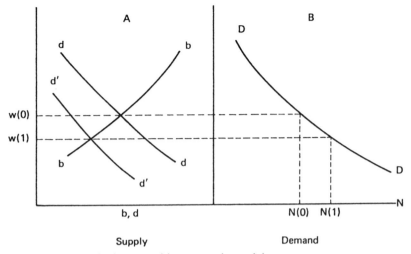

Figure I   A simple demographic-economic model
Note: bb and dd denote birth and death rates, DD is the demand for population, w
the real wage rate, and N population

population change at a zero rate. In Figure I supply and demand
are described in panels A and B. The wage w(0), which permits
population to 'tick over', is found where the death rate (dd) and
the birth rate (bb) cross. DD in panel B describes labour demand.
Here at the equilibrium population N(0) supply matches demand.
An exogenous shift to the system due to, say, a costless cure to
some disease (represented by dd in panel A) would have the
following effects: it would cut the wage to w(1), reduce both
nuptiality and mortality, and increase the equilibrium population
to N(1); while only a *lasting* increase in the demand for labour
would sustain a wage that would allow the birth rate to exceed the
death rate in the long run. In this view it is the failure of Irish AAM
to rise (i.e. of nuptiality to fall), given the exogenous shock to
mortality from smallpox inoculation, that is to be explained. In
Britain, industrialization holds the key to sustained population
growth; in Ireland, the potato and the buoyancy of the eighteenth-
century economy combined to keep wages high enough to guar-
antee earlier, high nuptiality levels. Hence a sustained higher
population growth rate was possible from 1750–1815. But after the
wartime boom, a reduction in the demand for labour combined
with further advances against smallpox had the net effect of

reducing both fertility and population growth, and also of preventing the death rate from rising.

(ii) Pre-Famine famines

It is natural to seek in the tea-leaves of pre-Famine history dire warnings of what lay in store. The long litany of pre-Famine famines prepared by William Wilde for the 1851 census commissioners, where they are depicted as previews of impending doom, is echoed in much of the literature (e.g. Grigg, 1980, *138*).[10] Yet a closer analysis of the record suggests that pre-blight famine mortality was relatively light. Not that Ireland was spared famine. The long cold spell of 1740 – Europe's worst on record (Post, 1985, *ch. 3*) – brought havoc to Ireland as elsewhere. Both root and cereal crops were destroyed, and the classic famine symptoms of roadside deaths, dysentery and typhus followed. The anonymous author of *The Groans of Ireland* described 'the most miserable scenes of universal distress that I ever read in history . . . the roads spread with dead and dying bodies; mankind of the colour of the docks and nettles which they fed on and many buried only in the fields and ditches where they perished' (quoted in Drake, 1968). Frost throughout most of the summer of 1740 made for a short growing season, and famine conditions persisted into 1741. The price of wheat on the Dublin market almost doubled and stayed high, while government did little beyond prohibiting grain exports and keeping the army in quarters. The soup kitchens and public works organized by landlords and others, often in commercialized, urban areas removed from the worst of the crisis, could not prevent massive mortality. The ensuing catastrophe, vividly described in many contemporary accounts, exacted a massive toll in lives. Estimates of mortality must be highly conjectural, but a recent tentative guess based on hearth tax data suggests a toll of 0.25 million. If correct, that crisis was in relative terms a greater killer than the Great Famine. The figure also implies that the crisis was deeper in Ireland than anywhere else in Europe, Norway excepted

---

[10]   *The Census of Ireland for the Year 1851*, Part V, *Tables of Deaths* H. C. 1856, xxix, p. 151; George O'Brien (1921) *The Economic History of Ireland from the Union to the Famine* (Dublin), pp. 222–31.

(Post, 1985). The proximate causes of death were the usual famine mix: first starvation, dysentry, and relapsing fever, then typhus fever. Typhus, which attacked both rich and poor, seems to have been rampant in 1741 (Post, 1985, *243–6*).

Notwithstanding the claims of Connell and Drake – who have associated the following half-century with a 'gap in famines' (Connell, 1950, Drake, 1963, *144–6*) – other subsistence crises followed. That of 1745–6 was severe in the north and west; other crises in 1755, 1766, and 1783 seem to have been more widely spread. But patchy and poor parish register data have so far precluded an assessment of mortality in those years. A few decades later, Ireland shared the crises of 1800–1 and 1816–19 with the rest of Europe, and in Ireland 1822 and 1830–1 are also listed as crisis years.

How do these different crises compare? A little informed guess-work is the best that one can do. Newenham thought the excess mortality in 1800–1 had been about 40,000. Excess mortality during the crisis of 1816–19, the most protracted and best-documented of the post-1800 crises, was put at 44,000 by Harty and at 65,000 by Barker and Cheyne, two Dublin medical men charged with public health at the time.[11] This may seem horrific enough, but it is tiny compared with the Great Famine, and indeed small compared with other parts of Europe. The 1816–19 crisis was augured in by a wet and cold summer in 1816. Distress was met by local relief committees, and private and public charity combined (in a ratio of about 10 to 1). Few starved before the summer of 1817, and that year's harvest was good, but typhus (or 'black fever') had already struck and remained endemic until 1819, peaking in the summer of 1818. The victims were mainly the poor but, as in 1741, the better-off were not immune from typhus either.[12]

In 1822 atrocious weather conditions brought the threat of famine again, and 10 western counties probably escaped serious

[11] Newenham, *Inquiry*, pp. 131–2; W. Harty (1820) *An Historic Sketch of the Progress, Extent and Mortality of the Contagious Fever Epidemic During the Years 1817, 1818 and 1819* (Dublin), p. 21; F. Barker and J. Cheyne (1821) *An Account of the Rise, Progress and Decline of the Fever Lately Epidemical in Ireland* (Dublin).
[12] Timothy O'Neill (1966) 'The Famine of 1822' (unpublished M.A. thesis, National University of Ireland), ch. 2.

mortality only because of impressive injections of relief. In the worst-hit counties of Clare, Galway, Mayo and Kerry public and private outlays combined exceeded £1 per family. Deaths were recorded in the west, yet detailed analysis suggests that in the end the number of lives lost in 1822 was few:[13] whether the crisis deserves the appellation of 'famine' is a moot point. This time, by contrast with a few years earlier, the crisis was short-lived and outbreaks of fever closely monitored.

Middle-class terror of typhus bred institutional palliatives. The crisis of 1801 had produced Dublin's House of Recovery, that of 1816–19 the Board of Health and the Mendicity Association. No real cure for famine fever was available, though, the 'remedy' being to quarantine those affected. Patients were 'conveyed to the house in a covered carriage placed on springs . . . stripped . . . washed in warm water, and . . . conveyed to bed'. But by no means all relief was so self-interested. In contrast to official attitudes at the height of the Great Famine, in 1817–19 Peel, now Home Secretary, fully accepted ultimate responsibility 'wherein no local exertion can be made'. The system of local relief committees devised in 1817–19 was used again in 1822 (Royle, 1984), and during the summer and autumn of that year there were thousands of them.[14] Relief works were also a feature, with particular emphasis on road-building and quays, market houses, harbours and jails. This marked Westminster's first intervention in the area. Private charity, both Irish and British, again played a very important part. The Famine of 1831 produced excess deaths in the west, but once more a major outbreak of typhus was avoided.

Recent research raises the possibility that subsistence crises in the years between the famines of 1740–1 and 1800 were at least as severe as those between 1800 and 1845 (Dickson, 1989). While all the crises listed cost lives, mass starvation was rare after 1745, and ironically almost absent in the run-up to 1845. The evidence of the Irish Poor Inquiry of 1835–6, and indeed Wilde's own work for the 1841 census commissioners, supports this. Both record starvation deaths, but not of the generalized sort associated with endemic

[13] *Report of the Committee for the Relief of the Distressed Districts in Ireland* (London, 1823), pp. 54–5. Over £0.5 million was expended on relief in 1822. For details see Timothy P. O'Neill (1971) 'The State, Poverty and Distress in Ireland, 1815–45' (unpublished Ph.D. thesis, National University of Ireland), p. 309.

[14] T. O'Neill, 'The Famine of 1822', p. 40.

famine. The 1841 census records only 117 cases of starvation during the 1830s in its mortality tables, an underestimate, but – even though literal starvation is never the main cause of excess deaths in famine conditions – a telling number nevertheless. The local experts consulted by the Poor Inquiry Commissioners indicate that most of those who succumbed to hunger in the early 1830s – again a small number – were individual vagrants and beggars. Should this come as a surprise, it must be because we are perhaps too readily convinced by retrospective, largely inferential, claims that famines were becoming more general before the Great Famine. Malthusian inference may suggest as much, but the historical record is more complex. On the flimsy evidence available, Irish reliance on the potato, in terms of the *ex ante* probability of disaster, may have been a relatively low-risk strategy (Ó Gráda, 1988, *ch. 1*; Solar, 1989).

The pre-harvest hunger highlighted by visitors to Ireland (most of whom toured in the summertime) and other observers must be distinguished from famine proper. This summer hunger, hallmark of pre-famine poverty, is still common in some underdeveloped countries today, but it made Ireland special among nineteenth-century western European nations. In years of famine or near-famine such as 1816 and 1822 seasonal dearth lasted four or five months, and risked becoming famine. Still, a combination of private charity and government aid was nearly always enough to stave off the worst before 1846.

(iii) The potato

A gift from the New World that probably reached Ireland via Spain about 1590, the potato has played a greater part in the history of Ireland than of any other European country.[15] This must surely be due to its comparative advantage in Ireland for climatic reasons over grain crops. The potato's early history in Ireland is very

---

[15] For some useful comparative perspective, see M. Drake (1969) *Population and Society in Norway 1735–1865* (Cambridge), pp. 54–65; M. Morineau (1970) 'La Pomme de Terre au 19ᵉ Siècle', *Annales E.S.C.* 25, translated in R. Forster and O. Ranum (eds), *Food and Drink in History* (Baltimore, 1979), pp. 17–36; M. Flinn et al. (1977) *Scottish Population History from the Seventeenth Century to the 1930s* (Cambridge), pp. 421–38.

unclear. The literary sources are confusing and sometimes contradictory (Cullen, 1968; Salaman, 1985). Thus political arithmetician Sir William Petty, who knew Ireland well, suggests in one place that 'six out of eight of all the Irish . . . feed chiefly upon milk and potatoes', but in another that 'their food is bread in cakes . . . potatoes from August till May, Muscles, Cockles and Oysters near the Sea; Eggs and Butter made very rancid'.[16] The literary evidence for early diffusion is strongest for Munster, but accounts from places as different as Connacht, Kilkenny and Derry suggest that the potato's victory in those areas was late. The diffusion mechanism is controversial too (Mokyr, 1981). Did the potato cause Ireland's population explosion, or vice versa? Against Connell and Drake's case for the potato as the engine driving population, Cullen allows the root only an accommodating role in sustaining a population increase already under way (Cullen, 1968). This fits his Boserupian (*) view of potato diffusion as a lagged response to demographic change.

Over time the character of the potato must have changed considerably. The varieties introduced from Latin America were used originally as seasonal garden crops; how they evolved into 'Irish potatoes', lasting 7–9 months of the year, remains a mystery. In George Rye's discussion of potato varieties (1730), one of the earliest on record, five kinds are listed. In the following decades dozens of varieties tailored to a range of soil and climatic conditions unknown in Latin America were tried, in an attempt to stretch the season and provide insurance against crop failure. Unlike Andean users, however, the Irish failed (if they ever attempted) to devise a means of storing buffer stocks from one year to the next. Still, experimentation increased the potato's advantages. A common strain in the historiography is that the potato reduced the probability of subsistence crises occurring below the risk existing in countries relying on grain alone (Drake, 1963). Risk-spreading through additional potato varieties is also part of the story. But the trend before the Famine was greater specialization in three or four varieties, especially in the notorious 'lumper', which produced a generous crop on inferior soils. In purely nutritional terms, the 'lumper' probably matched the 'cup' or even

---

[16] C. H. Hull (ed.) (1899) *Economic Writings of Sir William Petty* (London), pp. 156, 191.

the 'apple', but its size and rather bland taste geared it towards pigs and cattle. Still its infamy, resting largely on its allegedly weaker resistance to blight, is not totally deserved. Its record before 1845 was good, and *all* late varieties succumbed to blight in 1845. Indeed, one of the early selling points of the 'lumper' was its immunity to curl, a plant disease that did not spare other varieties. In a series of experiments carried out in Scotland less than a decade before the Famine the 'lumper' outperformed over 130 other varieties for its yield, reliability, and leaching properties.[17]

The insurance provided by the potato fell as its preponderance in the diet of the poor rose. Still, an analysis of the early variation in crop yields suggests that the statistical probability of once-off major failure was small and before *Phytophthera infestans*, a two- or three-time failure utterly improbable (Solar, 1989). The potato's dual role as human food and fodder crop – only one-half of average output ended up in human stomachs – raises one of its saving graces: it was the farmyard pig and hen who bore the brunt of mild scarcities.

Ireland's official agricultural statistics began at the height of the Famine in 1847, when the area under potatoes had shrivelled to less than 0.3 million acres. The extent of the potato's diffusion on the eve of the Famine is a much trickier question, but a figure of over 2 million acres seems plausible (Crotty, 1966; Bourke, 1968; Mokyr, 1981). Potatoes thus seem to have accounted for about one-third of all tilled land. Potato ground was farmed with great care; spade cultivation produced deep ridges, and generous doses of lime, manure, and seasand – carried for great distances when necessary – nourished the seed. Consequently, yields per acre were high. There were enough potatoes in most years to feed the 3 million or so who consumed little else, the rest of the population who also consumed large quantities, and the pigs and fowls for whom the root was also the main food. For an adult male to consume 12–14 lbs (or 5–6 kilos) of potatoes daily for most of the year, and the rest of his family in proportion, seems today like a feat worthy of the *Guinness Book of Records*. 'The Englishman', noted a contemporary, 'would find considerable difficulty in

---

[17] A. Howden (1837) 'Reports of Experiments on the Comparative Value of Different Varieties of Potato', *Transactions of the Highland and Agricultural Society of Scotland*, XI.

Table 1.2 *Allocation of the potato crop, c. 1845 (in million tons)*

A.	Human consumption in Ireland:		
	Occupation	Population	Annual consumption
	Labourers	3.3	3.9
	Cottiers	1.4	0.8
	Small farmers	0.5	0.3
	Large farmers	0.25	0.1
	Textile workers	0.75	0.4
	Other workers	0.85	0.4
	Professional and other	0.95	0.3
	Total	8.2	6.2
B.	Animal consumption:		
	Pigs		2.6
	Cattle		1.8
	Horses and other		0.3
C.	Exports:		0.2
D.	Seed and wastage:		2.5

Source: (Bourke, 1968) slightly amended.

stowing away in his stomach this enormous quantity of vegetable food, and how an Irishman is able to manage it is beyond my ability to explain' (quoted in Bourke, 1968, 76). Table 1.2, adapted from Bourke, explains the allocation of the root.[18] It shows that while the potato was the food of the poor, *par excellence*, its consumption was impressive further up the social scale too (compare Cullen, 1981). The Irish *enjoyed* their potatoes, and it is a safe guess that varieties in common use before the Famine – the 'lumper' apart – were much tastier than the bland potatoes commonly available today.

The potato is the most versatile food known to man. Modern dietary analysis suggests that the Irishman's gargantuan meals of potatoes and buttermilk provided all the proteins, calories and minerals he needed. Table 1.3, based on a comparison of the typical labourers' diet in 1839 with a modern Canadian estimate of dietary requirements, makes the point. In strictly nutritional terms

[18] In order to square Bourke's numbers with Mokyr's revisions (Mokyr, 1981), these consumption levels have been allowed for ten months of the year only.

Table 1.3 *The nutritional quality of the pre-Famine potato diet*

Dietary measure	Actual, Ireland 1839	Recommended today for active males 25–49 years
Protein	134.6	61
Fat	3.6	not given
Carbohydrate	1099.1	not given
Energy value	4720	2700
Calcium	2398	800
Iron	24.5	8

Note: Protein, fat and carbohydrate intake are measured in grams, energy value in kcals, and calcium and iron in milligrams.
Source: The 1839 data are taken from (Clarkson and Crawford, 1988), the modern data from *Recommended Nutrient Intakes for Canadians* (Ottawa, 1983).

the simple Irish fare was fine, being deficient only in vitamins A and D. A boon of the humble potato was that it shielded the Irish poor from afflictions such as scurvy – 'the very rarest of diseases in Ireland' (Crawford, 1984, *155*) – and xerophthalmia. Pellagra, too, endemic long after in those parts of the southern United States and Europe in which maize was the staple, was rare in Ireland. The most careful assessment to date of Irish diets on the eve of the Famine suggests that they were 'excellent, not merely when measured by "recommended daily intake" of the nutritionist, but also when set against the historical reality of the later nineteenth century' (Clarkson and Crawford, 1988, *191*).

The poor, it is true, consumed quantities of other foods besides. Milk was a seasonal supplement, and oatmeal was widely consumed in the north and east. Herrings were also widely available: about one-quarter of the Irish Poor Inquiry's informants in 1835–6 mention them. Other regional variations emerge from recent research. Eggs were apparently consumed in some quantities by the western poor before the Famine, and the role of bread and bacon in the urban diet comes as no surprise. Still, it is the potato's domination that is most strikingly confirmed (Clarkson and Crawford, 1988).

On the eve of the Famine, across most of Ireland the potato was at the same time the labourer's staple and a crucial element in the agricultural system that had evolved since the mid-eighteenth century. Much like the turnip in England, the potato's role in the rotation was to cleanse the soil and prevent leaching, tasks it fulfilled without reducing the earth's nitrogen content. Hence the readiness of the farmer to risk letting heavily-manured plots of potato-land (called conacre) to their workers in a system that in practice amounted to bonded labour. The potato played an important part in the peculiar revolution in Irish agriculture which gradually converted the country into a kind of granary for the rest of the United Kingdom. The potato's shortcomings are familiar too. So low was its value-to-weight ratio before the Famine that transporting it overland caused its value to 'evaporate' at a rate of over 2 per cent per mile. Storage was cheap in the sense that it required no capital equipment – pits or clamps covered with straw were enough. But the marked seasonality in potato prices, a rise of about 30 per cent from trough to peak, compared with less than half that for cereals, suggests that the cost in terms of food value loss was quite high (Hoffman and Mokyr, 1983; Ó Gráda, 1988).

(iv) Economic trends before 1845

The demographic history of Ireland is better known than its economic history. The economic history of the pre-Famine decades, in particular, was long neglected, but in recent years it has attracted several able scholars, mainly American (see *Bibliography*, items 1; 11; 59; 60; 61; 69; 79; 80). The broad outlines of economic trends are becoming clear. Recent research has replaced the traditional preoccupation with legal and institutional factors by models in which the impact of the Industrial Revolution is paramount. In the pre-Famine decades, the shift in comparative advantage produced by the Industrial Revolution is judged to have forced Ireland to concentrate less on manufacturing and more on agriculture. Since the price of food continued to rise relative to industrial prices, one consequence was an improvement in Ireland's terms of trade (*). This added to Ireland's aggregate income. However, food bulked so large in the budgets of the landless masses that the shift in the terms of trade meant immiseration for them. The point is important. In much of the west and even in Ulster outside the 'linen triangle' linking the towns of Belfast, Dungannon and Lurgan, Irish cottage industry waned from the 1810s on. Elsewhere in Ireland the First Industrial Revolution in England seemed to rule out industrialization as a solution to poverty. This increased the vulnerability of the poor to harvest failure, and thus the Famine may be seen, in part at least, as the outcome of an industrial crisis (Ó Gráda, 1984).

Exactly why comparative advantage dictated industrial decline for Ireland is still unclear. Since the theory of comparative advantage refers to *two* economies and *two* commodities, it cannot be supported on Irish evidence alone. Irish wages were notoriously low, but they failed, by and large, to attract modern industry. Indeed, within Ireland, it was a relatively high-wage region, the north-east, which industrialized more in the pre-Famine decades. Thus the model applied by Mokyr (*Industrialization in the Low Countries*, 1976) to nineteenth-century Belgium and Holland, whereby the region with the cheaper labour (Belgium) industrialized first, fails in the Irish case. Nor is the notion that violent crime deterred entrepreneurs from investing very convincing, because attacks on industrialists and industrial capital in pre-Famine Ireland were rare. Another explanation for the failure to industrialize, Ireland's lack of natural resources such as coal and iron, was rejected by Robert Kane as long ago as 1844, Kane argued that importing them would have added little to total costs. The experience of neither England nor Benelux seems to support Kane, however; the location of industries *within* those areas suggests that they were far less footloose than Kane allowed (Mokyr, 1983, *153–4*).

The hypothesis that external economies (*) in the manufacturing sector dictated the centralization of industrial capital in Britain is the most plausible, but the most difficult to prove. It is at least consistent with both the localization of the cotton industry within ever-smaller regions of England and Scotland, and the concentration of the linen and ancillary industries around Belfast. Before the Famine textile towns such as Drogheda, Bandon, and Kilkenny were hard hit by the competition of imports from England; and cottage industry in remoter rural areas also suffered. Only linen, in retrospect a poor prospect compared to cotton or worsteds, advanced, and that in only a small area in the north-east (Kennedy and Ollerenshaw, 1985, *3–16*). The vast increase in Irish food exports between Union and Famine was prompted by an improvement in Ireland's terms of trade. This increase was accompanied by impressive gains in the allied sectors of food processing, banking, and communications. In the pre-Famine decades Ireland's flour mills rivalled for size and technical ingenuity the cotton mills of Lancashire, its banking system was thoroughly revolutionized along joint-stock lines, and steamships and a well-coordinated network of roads cut fares and travel time. The Famine has tended to overshadow these considerable achievements.

Even agriculture progressed, though by how much is controversial. One thing seems certain: only a hefty dose of ingenuity could have generated both the rise in exports and the extra food needed to feed a population that more than doubled between Arthur Young's time and the Famine. Some of the rise in exports must have been at the expense of domestic consumption; though how much is an unresolved issue. Still, in view of a historiographical tradition which maintains that the Irish agriculturalist was either too shiftless to achieve much or too persecuted to be industrious, the most significant point is that mass starvation was avoided for so long. The Law of Diminishing Returns, a key feature of the Malthusian presumption that food supply could not keep pace with a fast-growing population, was at least held at bay. How? The diffusion of new techniques developed in Britain is one factor: contemporary evidence shows that wheeled carts, ploughs, new seed varieties, and modern rotations were making inroads in all but the remotest pockets of Ireland, and that larger farmers had been thoroughly won over by the 1840s. The maldistribution of farmland – on the eve of the Famine one-third of landholders farmed two-thirds or more of the land – suggests that most of Irish agriculture was affected. Grain yields per acre rose between the time of Arthur Young, whose *Tour in Ireland* (1776–8) provides the earliest estimates by region, and the early 1840s. Some of this rise was doubtless due to increasing labour intensity, but that is far from being the whole story.[19] Improvements in estate management may have helped too. As landowners took a more direct interest in their properties, they hired energetic agents, conducted surveys,

[19] See R. C. Allen and C. Ó Gráda (1988) 'On the Road Again With Arthur Young: English, Irish and French Agriculture During the Industrial Revolution', *Journal of Economic History*, XLVII (March).

and squeezed out middlemen. However, such vigour probably resulted more in the redistribution of the economic rent towards landlords than in higher output. And yet, agricultural output per worker in Ireland was only about one-half that in Britain in 1845. Resource constraints rather than laziness or inefficiency may well have been responsible for this gap (Ó Gráda, 1988, *ch. 2*). The improvement in output was not enough to prevent the living standards of the poor from falling. On the eve of the Famine the poverty of Irish smallholding and labouring families, a rising share of total population, was legendary. The poor were wretchedly housed – two-thirds of the entire population huddled into sparsely furnished, tiny mud cottages or their urban equivalents – and poorly clothed, and often hungry for two or three months of every year. Yet not quite all was gloom and doom. In much of the country the worst effects of the poor clothing and housing were mitigated by cheap and abundant fuel in the form of peat. From army recruitment and prison data, it appears that the Irish poor were sturdy and relatively tall. Besides, life expectancy in Ireland was respectable by contemporary standards: at 37 or 38 years, it lagged somewhat behind England or Scandinavia, but was probably higher than most other places in Europe (Boyle and Ó Gráda, 1986). Yet the Irish poor, given the choice, might well have traded an extra few years of life on the potato for the more intense pleasures of bread and tea.

The outpouring of official documentation about Ireland after the Union bespeaks increasing official awareness of its problems. Indeed, the 'blue books' of the day provide brilliant economic and social surveys of Ireland for the historian studying the period. The great official inquiries of the 1830–45 period – those on education, railways, poverty, and land tenure – revealed to policy-makers a new 'hidden Ireland', yet they failed to generate dramatic structural change. The Irish Poor Inquiry, conducted in the wake of its more famous English counterpart, rejected the workhouse as a solution to poverty. Instead Archbishop Whately and his fellow-commissioners emphasized investment and public involvement. The contrast between this report and that of Senior and Chadwick on the Old Poor Law in England is remarkable. The English report of 1834, a paean to self-help and economy, had dwelt on (and exaggerated) the alleged evils of a system of public charity already in being. To the chagrin of ministers, the Irish report virtually ignored this message, and its findings were rejected by the British government as too radical. George Nicholls, one of the original English commissioners, was sent off to prepare a more palatable report, ignoring 'the plans for the general improvement of Ireland contained in the report of the commissioners of inquiry'. Nicholls reported within six weeks, concluding that the English model would work in Ireland. This was acted on. The Irish Poor Law was certainly no developmental panacea, but it marked the most ambitious administrative reform yet attempted in Ireland, and one which was to be relied on greatly during the Famine.

By 1845 the last of the planned 130 workhouses had been built, and nearly all were receiving paupers. The Irish Poor Law followed closely the new English model of 1834. The cardinal principle of 'less eligibility' was imposed by discipline, work, isolation from family members, and dull food given sparingly. The system worked in the sense that the poor rates were collected and the workhouses were not immediately inundated to capacity by paupers. By 1843 there was accommodation for 100,000 inmates, but the workhouses rarely held more than 40,000 at any one time before the Famine. Indeed proportionately fewer paupers resorted to workhouses in Ireland than did paupers in England before 1845. The system's architects thus need not have fretted about able-bodied malingerers bankrupting the ratepayers. Those who entered were indeed true hardship cases, without material support. In the spring of 1844, for example, only three-fifths of the inmates were of working age, and one-third were deemed in bad health on entry. The workhouse test worked at a cost of making life almost intolerable for the unfortunates who passed it (O'Brien, 1985). The diet varied slightly from place to place, being best in east Ulster, where wages were highest. This system would be forced to bear the brunt of relief during much of the Famine.

Some have detected in the post-1830 legislative package in Ireland – a package that included free elementary education, the Poor Law, and public health measures – the timid beginnings of an Irish welfare state. But the motives of Irish Under-Secretary Thomas Drummond or Lord Melbourne were not those of, say, Aneurin Bevan or Lord Beveridge. No government before 1845 envisaged the betterment of the poor through a mass transfer of resources from the rich. Indeed in an influential Whig manifesto published on the eve of the Famine the boldest measure advocated was the payment of the Catholic priesthood.[20] Welfare apart, more public spending on education, emigration, and railways would have reduced Irish vulnerability. Subsidized emigration was proposed by the Emigration Commissioners in 1826, by the Poor Inquiry Commissioners in 1836, the Devon Commission in 1845, and by several independent experts, but all for nought. Governments reasoned that they could handle emergencies through short-term relief measures.

(v) So 'was Malthus right' (Mokyr, 1983)?

Indirectly through his ideas rather than directly through what he wrote about Ireland, Malthus is the key to pre-Famine population historiography. Implicitly or explicitly, increasing Irish poverty has been put down to 'the vortex of subdivision and early marriage', and the Great Famine seen as 'the ultimate Malthusian catastrophe'.[21] In time series perspective, the association between rising population and impoverishment seems undeniable. The inexorable effect of the Law of Diminishing Returns may be observed in the apparent tendency of the economy to be grinding to a halt in the 1830s. Grain exports to Great Britain, for example, averaged 491,000 tons in 1836–8, but only 356,000 tons in 1839–42, and 463,000 tons in 1843–5 (Donnelly, 1972, *32–3*).[22] Merchandise traffic along the country's waterways was also sluggish in these years. And not only were rising numbers apparently adding little to output: the pressure on living standards was in turn forcing population growth to slacken. Moreover, there is the authority of Malthus himself, who in a famous passage in the *Essay on Popula-*

[20] Nassau Senior, 'Ireland in 1843', first published in the *Edinburgh Review*, in 1843, reprinted in Senior's *Journals, Essays and Conversations Relating to Ireland* (2 vols, London, 1868), vol. 1. Senior's correspondence with Macvey Napier, editor of the *Edinburgh* (B.L. Add. Mss. 34623, f622.) shows that his article was cleared by the Whig leadership before publication.

[21] Oliver MacDonagh (1970) *The Nineteenth Century Novel and Irish Social History: Some Aspects* (Dublin), p. 7.

[22] But, as Donnelly (p. *33*) points out, a series of very poor grain and potato harvests after 1839 diverted some output to domestic consumption. The export data therefore exaggerate the effect of diminishing returns.

tion of 1798 outlines the Third Horseman's role as ultimate positive check:

Famine seems to be the last, the most dreadful resource of nature. The power of population is so superior to the power of the earth to produce subsistence for man, that premature death must in some shape or other visit the human race. The vices of mankind are active and able ministers of depopulation. They are the precursors in the great army of destruction; and often finish the dreadful work themselves. But should they fail in this war of extermination, sickly seasons, epidemics, pestilence, and plague, advance in terrific array, and sweep off their thousands and tens of thousands. Should success be still incomplete, gigantic inevitable famine stalks in the rear, and with one mighty blow levels the population with the food of the world.[23]

That passage, although not related to Ireland, reads like a prophetic rendition of later assessments. But if the Irish mini-famines of 1800–1 and 1816–19 are interpreted in this light, they failed in their mission to halt population growth. In this, they fit a common pattern. The broad historical record suggests that, though other positive checks played a role, famine was not the main mechanism for maintaining a balance between population and food supply in the past (Watkins and Menken, 1985). The Great Famine is a different story. Oddly enough, though, it is not the future that Malthus foresaw for Ireland on the only occasion that he wrote at length about it. In an anonymous essay in the *Edinburgh Review*,[24] he predicted instead:

Although it is quite certain that the population of Ireland cannot continue permanently to increase at its present rate, yet it is as certain that it will not *suddenly* come to a stop . . . Both theory and experience uniformly instruct us, that a less abundant supply of food operates with a gradually increasing pressure for a long time before its progress is stopt. It is difficult indeed to conceive a more tremendous shock to society, than the event of its coming at once to the limits of the means of subsistence, with all the habits of abundance and early marriages that accompany a rapidly increasing population. But, happily for mankind, this never is, not even can be the case. The event is provided for by the concurrent interests and feelings of individuals long before it arrives; and the gradual diminution of the real

---

[23] Thomas Robert Malthus (1970) *Essay on the Principle of Population* (Pelican edn, Harmondsworth), pp. 118–19.
[24] Anon. (T. R. Malthus), 'Newenham and Others on the State of Ireland', *Edinburgh Review* July 1808, reprinted in B. Semmel (ed.), *Occasional Papers of T. R. Malthus* (New York, 1963), p. 42.

wages of the labouring classes of society, slowly, almost insensibly, generates the habits necessary for an order of things in which the funds for the maintenance of labour are stationary.

Malthus thus ruled out 'gigantic, inevitable famine' as a cure for Irish overpopulation. The contrast between these passages captures in microcosm the shift in his position between the original edition of the *Essay on Population* and the second, 'which soften(s) some of the harshest conclusions' of the first. But quoting Malthus against Malthus is not enough. By and large, both Irish historiography and Malthusian exegesis have accepted the 'positive check' version of the Malthusian model (Grigg, 1980, *115–40*; Ó Gráda, 1984). The outstanding exception is Joel Mokyr's *Why Ireland Starved* (1983/85). This major work, revolutionary in scope and method, has cast a cold cliometric eye on Malthusian orthodoxy, and found it wanting. Mokyr's approach is to test the proposition 'was Malthus right?' through use of econometric techniques, by focusing on the effect of the land/labour ratio on living standards.

Ideally, to test the Malthusian hypothesis requires time series of population, and other variables such as land quality, and non-agricultural employment (Table 1.4). Such data are lacking for pre-Famine Ireland. Mokyr, therefore, first creates new economic and demographic data for all 32 counties on the eve of the Famine from sources such as the Poor Inquiry, the 1841 Census, and the Devon Commission. He then treats the counties *c.*1845 as so many hypothetical observations in time, thus ingeniously circumventing the absence of time-series data. All his cross-section regressions of income on land/labour ratio variables return a broadly negative verdict on the central proposition. The results reported in Table 1.4 are typical. Three different land-quality variables are reported. Broadly speaking the explanatory, or control, variables perform as expected; income rises with the capital/labour ratio, and falls with the poverty of housing (Mokyr defines Housing Quality inversely, as the proportion of housing in the lowest quality category in the 1841 census). But the outcome hardly supports the Malthusian hypothesis, since, crucially, the population pressure variable (defined throughout as the rural land/labour ratio) has the incorrect (i.e. negative) sign. Nor can 'economic' variables (such as Income Per Capita, Cottage Industry, Housing Quality) explain

Table 1.4 *Testing for 'overpopulation' in Ireland c. 1845*

| | | Dependent variable | | |
| | | Column 1 | Column 2 | Column 3 |
Explanatory variables		Income per head	Wage	Wage
Row 1	Population pressure	−0.72 (−1.67)	−0.35 (−1.63)	−1.02 (−2.65)
Row 2	Land quality Index[a]	−0.31 (−1.58)	0.06 (0.43)	1.62 (3.08)
Row 3	Capital/ labour ratio	1.35 (5.35)	0.42 (4.29)	1.49 (6.80)
Row 4	Literacy	1.41 (0.72)	0.80 (0.94)	−1.02 (−0.57)
Row 5	Housing quality	−4.14 (−3.26)	−1.82 (−2.95)	−3.34 (−2.86)
Row 6	Cottage industry		2.25 (3.18)	
Row 7	Proportion manufacturing	1.10 (0.80)		1.85 (1.48)
Row 8	Percentage urban	4.86 (5.59)	2.44 (4.12)	4.93 (6.39)
Row 9	F (7, 24)	45.74	26.24	58.74

Source: (Mokyr, revised edn, 1985: 49).
[a] Three versions of this variable are used. See note below.

Notes for the Econometrically Uninitiated
This table summarizes the results of multiple regression equations designed to test the Malthusian hypothesis. As explained in the text, for this purpose we need, ideally, time-series data (e.g. data running from, say, 1700 to 1850) for population, income, etc., but for most variables we lack evidence of this kind. Mokyr has therefore created data for each of the 32 counties of Ireland using evidence from the 1836 Poor Inquiry, the 1841 Census, etc. He then treats the data as though they were time-series data. That is to say, the 32 counties of Ireland, which were at different levels of development on the eve of the Famine, are regarded as representing different stages of the Irish economy at consecutive points in time.

The purpose of multiple regression analysis is to establish a relationship between the behaviour of one variable (say, income) and the combined behaviour of other variables (say, land per head of population, the quality of land, etc.). In the table above the values of TEN variables are presented. TWO of the variables are *dependent variables* which have to be 'explained' and EIGHT are *explanatory variables* that do the explaining. (One of the dependent variables – wage – is 'explained' in two different ways: hence the two columns headed 'wage'.)

The Dependent Variables
Column 1: Income per head.
Column 2: Wage.
Column 3: Wage.

The Explanatory Variables
Row 1: Population pressure
The *population pressure* variable measures how much rural land is available in a county per head of population.
Row 2: Land quality index
The *land quality index* exists in three versions:
    (i) variance of the altitude of land in a county above sea level;
    (ii) mean altitude of land in a county above sea level;
    (iii) proportion of land in a county under cultivation.
Row 3: Capital/labour ratio
Row 4: Literary
Row 5: Housing quality
Housing quality is defined as the proportion of housing in the lowest quality category in the 1841 census.
Row 6: Cottage industry
Row 7: Percentage of the population in manufacturing
The variables presented in *Rows 6 and 7* are alternative measures of the same characteristic. The former is employed in the calculations in *Column 2* and the latter in *Column 3*.
Row 8: Proportion of the population in towns

The *Explanatory Variables* are used in the following way:
    (a) Column 1 'explains' *income per head* in terms of the *land quality index*, version (i) and six other variables.
    (b) *Column 2* 'explains' *wage* in terms of the *land quality index*, version (ii) and six other variables.
    (c) *Column 3* 'explains' *wage* in terms of the *land quality index*, version (iii) and six other variables.

Interpretations
The table should be interpreted in the following manner.
Row 1 This row suggests that the more land a person has (the *population pressure* variable), the *lower* his *income* or *wage* (the signs are negative). This is true whatever index of *land quality* is used. This is contrary to the Malthusian hypothesis which postulates that the more land a person has the *higher* will be his income or wage.

Row 2 suggests that *land quality* had no clear effect on *income per head* or *wage*, although the proportion of land under cultivation seems to be quite strongly positively correlated to *wage*.

Row 3 suggests that the higher the *capital/labour ratio* the higher will be *income per head* or *wage*.

Row 4 suggests rather ambiguous connections between literacy and *income per head* or *wage*.

Row 5 suggests that the poorer the housing the lower the *income per head* or *wage*.

Row 6 suggests that the more *cottage industry* the higher the *wage*.

Row 7 suggests that the greater the proportion of the population in *manufacturing* the greater will be *income per head*.

Row 8 shows that *income per head* or *wage* is greater in counties which have a higher proportion of their populations living in towns than those with a lower proportion.

Technical Note
(a) The figures in brackets in *Rows 1–8* are the T-statistics and are measures of the reliability of the findings reported in each cell of the table; they show whether or not the results have occurred by chance. For a discussion see any introductory textbook of econometrics, e.g. Stewart and K. Wallis, *An Introductory Econometrics* (2nd edn, London, 1986). The T-statistics presented here confirm that the results in the table did not arise by chance.
(b) *Row 9* gives the results of the F-test. This is a further indication of how much confidence we can place on the relationships revealed by regression analysis. The F statistics presented here confirm that the results in the table did not arise by chance.

much of the cross-country variation in fertility or, more generally, population growth (Mokyr, 1983, *52–64*).

Hardly surprisingly, these results have provoked both keen interest and scepticism, though they have not been subjected so far to thorough testing (Kennedy, 1983; Solar, 1984). Criticism has focused on Mokyr's calculations of county income, but his results survive the correction of an error in the income estimates in the original edition. The validity of the cross-section approach rests crucially on the poor integration of the pre-Famine economy, because the counties are treated as *independent* observations of the effect of growing numbers on income. But is the implication of not one or two, but of 32 'county-economies' plausible? In support, Mokyr refers to the low mobility of labour between counties: in 1841 only 3 per cent of the population lived in counties other than where they were born (Mokyr, 1983, *45*). Here is an issue worth further study, since emigration and seasonal migration may have partly substituted for inter-county mobility. Poor wage data prevent a direct test of labour market integration, though the markets for goods and land seem to have been fairly well integrated (Kennedy, 1983). On the eve of the Famine the rent charged for land of given quality did not vary much across counties. Kennedy and McGregor[25] find that exogenous land quality variables account for over one-half of the cross-county variation in rent per acre; this suggests a well-integrated land market. Kennedy and McGregor's assessment is that it is too soon for firm verdicts against Malthus based on cross-section evidence. In the end, whether due to overpopulation or other factors, there is no denying the gradual decline in the living standards of the poor, the bottom half or so of the

[25] L. Kennedy and P. McGregor (1987) 'The Structure of the Pre-Famine Economy: A Preliminary Analysis' (unpublished).

population before 1845.[26] The shock of *Phytophthera infestans* would have had less of an impact in an economy with a larger margin to spare.

[26] J. Mokyr and C. Ó Gráda (1988), 'Poor and Getting Poorer? Irish Living Standards Before the Great Famine', *Economic History Review*, 2nd ser., XLI, May, pp. 209–35.

2

The Great Hunger 1845–1850

The arrival of *Phytophthera infestans* or potato blight in Ireland was first noted in the press on 6 September 1845. The 'New Disease' had already struck in the US in the summer of 1843. According to a contemporary account from there, 'potatoes [were] subject to dry rot, attacking some in the hill, and some in the heap, and fatal to the whole wherever it makes its appearance, causing them to rot and emit a very offensive stench'.[27] The blight then crossed the ocean by a mysterious route, reaching Ireland via Continental Europe and England. The news that Ireland had been hit caused the London *Gardener's Chronicle* to stop press, but local reports from Ireland were initially reassuring. Reaction in financial and commodity markets was minimal. Indeed the movement of potato prices on the Dublin market in the autumn of 1845 reflects this. Lumpers, which fetched 16d. to 20d. per hundredweight (or 50 kilos) in the second week of September, could still be bought for less than 18d. until near the end of November. (Then, it is true, prices rose beyond 2 shillings, and had passed 3 shillings by April 1846.) In political circles, however, the gravity of the situation soon became a 'party' issue: 'to profess belief in . . . the existence of a formidable potato blight, was as sure a method of being branded a radical, as to propose to destroy the Church'.[28] Constabulary crop returns soon put an end to the confusion; they suggested that less than half the crop had been lost, though the poor, who tended to plant their potatoes late, were worst hit.

---

[27] Quoted in N. E. Stevens (1933) 'The Dark Ages in Plant Pathology in America', *Journal of the Washington Academy of Sciences*, 23 (15 September), 441.

[28] (Isaac Butt) (1847) 'The Famine in the Land', *Dublin University Magazine*, vol. 29, 502.

The disease was, of course, a mystery. Most botanists agreed with Professor Lindley, eminent editor of the *Gardener's Chronicle*, who blamed the still, damp weather for the excess moisture that caused the tubers to rot. A fungal specialist, Rev. M. J. Berkeley, correctly diagnosed the mould on the plants as a 'vampire' fungus that fed on healthy potatoes, but the fungal hypothesis was scoffed at by most experts. Lindley dominated the official committee of inquiry ordered by Peel, now Prime Minister, and so the disease was diagnosed as a kind of wet rot. The committee's report suggested storage in well-ventilated pits as the best remedy: corollary remedies included dousing in quicklime, exposure to air, kiln drying, and a cover of ashes.[29] The blight excited enormous interest in the gardening and scientific press for a time, but Bourke (1964) suggests that 'few authentic clues' stand out amid the welter of hunches and assertions. Not that a different diagnosis would have eliminated the problem: an antidote for potato blight (copper sulphate solution) was not discovered until 1882. (Ironically the salutory effect of copper had been noted in Swansea in 1846, but quickly forgotten.) Acceptance of Berkeley's diagnosis would have dictated felling diseased tubers, thereby delaying the blight's progress. But that would not have mattered much. More important, the blight which, as noted above, had severely damaged the US potato crop in 1843, did so again in the US in 1844 and 1845 (Bourke, 1962). Had the fungal diagnosis been more widely accepted, might this tendency for the disease to recur have reduced the widespread complacency about the prospects of the 1846 Irish potato harvest?

Sir Robert Peel, long familiar with Irish problems – he had been Irish Secretary in 1822 and Home Secretary subsequently – acted quickly (O'Rourke, 1902, *122–30*). Against Treasury advice, he engaged the merchant house of Baring Brothers in November 1845 to purchase £100,000 worth of maize and meal – enough to feed 1 million people for over a month – in America. A buffer stock was built without fuss or publicity. In the event, it was hardly needed. Though history books often date the Famine from the first onslaught of the blight, few people perished in the 1845–6 season. This remarkable achievement was partly due to the efficacy of

---

[29]   P. Hickey (1980) 'A Study of Four Peninsular Parishes in West Cork 1796–1855' (Ph.D. thesis, National University of Ireland), pp. 303–11.

relief, but partly too to the country's ability to handle such a shortfall, provided the next year's crop was not long delayed.

(i) Chronology

The renewed and more complete failure of the potato in 1846 heralded the true beginning of the Great Famine. Another failure had not been anticipated, for despite the previous year's poor harvest, the potato acreage was close to an all-time high in 1846. In the early summer the potato plots bloomed 'like flower gardens', but any hopes that the blight might prove a one-year wonder soon vanished. The tell-tale discoloured leaves and stalks and the stench were everywhere, and another police report based on returns from all over the country put the average yield at less than half a ton per acre (compared to the usual six to seven tons). The prices of potatoes of all varieties rocketed. Cups, which had been worth less than 2 shillings per hundredweight (or 50 kilos) on the Dublin market in October 1845 were selling for over 7 shillings a year later, while the price of the lowly Lumper had jumped from about 16d. to 6 shillings.[30] The average agricultural wage per day was now less than the cost of a poor man's food, making no allowance for those dependent on him. Famine loomed. The new minority Whig administration of Lord John Russell faced urgent pleas for public works and controls on the grain trade. But having berated the Tories for over-reacting in 1845–6, Russell's policy was one of wait-and-see.

The numbers starving to death began to mount alarmingly in the autumn of 1846, and reports of some particularly gruesome cases soon began to appear in the press. Some of these are described at length by Woodham-Smith (1962) and Kee (1981), but in the retreat from 'emotiveness' mentioned earlier, other accounts shun them.[31] Yet reports such as the following pair from south-west Cork, usually considered the worst-hit area in the early stages of

[30] This did not result in higher potato consumption. The Famine thus produced no evidence for potatoes being a 'Giffen' (*) good (see Dwyer and Lindsay, 1984).

[31] Daly's otherwise excellent survey (Daly, 1986) omits such accounts entirely. In this, it reflects the dispassionate, sanitized approach to the Great Famine now dominant in Irish historical scholarship.

the Famine, are at the heart of the famine story. They make it 'a palpable thing', adding context to the matchstick scavengers portrayed in the *Illustrated London News* in 1847 and 1848, and widely reproduced since (Edwards and Williams, 1956; Irish University Press, 'Famine Series', 1968; Woodham-Smith, 1962):[32]

The famine grew more horrible towards the end of December 1846, many were buried with neither inquest nor coffin. An inquest was held by Dr. Sweetman on three bodies. The first was that of the father of two very young children whose mother had already died of starvation. His death became known only when the two children toddled into the village of Schull. They were crying of hunger and complaining that their father would not speak to them for four days; they told how he was 'as cold as a flag'. The other bodies on which an inquest was held were those of a mother and child who had both died of starvation. The remains had been gnawed by rats.

Other accounts, like this horrific report from Caheragh in the Cork *Southern Reporter*, were widely publicized:

The following is a statement of what I *saw* yesterday evening on the lands of Toureen. In a cabbage garden I saw (as I was informed) the bodies of Kate Barry and her two children very lightly covered with earth, the hands and legs of her large body entirely exposed, the flesh completely eaten off by the dogs, the skin and hair of the head lying within a couple of yards of the skull, which, when I first threw my eyes on it, I though to be part of a horse's tail. Within about thirty yards of the above-mentioned garden, at the opposite side of the road, are two most wretched-looking old houses, with two dead bodies in each, Norry Regan, Tom Barry, Nelly Barry (a little girl), and Charles McCarthy (a little boy), all dead about a fortnight, and not yet interred; Tim Donovan, Darrig, on the same farm, died on Saturday, his wife and sister the only people I saw about the cabin, said they had no means to bury him. You will think this very horrifying; but were you to witness the state of the dead and dying here at Toureen, it would be too much for flesh and blood to behold. May the Lord avert, by his gracious interposition, the merited tokens of his displeasure.

I need make no comment on this, but ask, *are we living in a portion of the United Kingdom?* (emphasis in the original)

Soon notices of 'deaths by starvation' lost their newsworthiness. The contemporary shock value of testimony such as that just quoted is difficult to evaluate. A generation ago the right-wing

[32] Hickey, *op. cit.*, p. 361.

historian Max Hartwell ventured that people like himself 'we: disciplined by familiarity with concentration camps' are left 'com paratively unmoved' by the scandal of child labour during th: Industrial Revolution.[33] The assessment of 'emotive' accounts o Famine starvation in Irish historiography is similar: contemporary policy-makers, inured to – and constrained by – mass misery, took them in their stride, and no more should be expected of them. Later generations, then, should not set anachronistically high standards for the politicians and bureaucrats of the 1840s. But this perspective ignores the fact that in Ireland most decent people were shocked (compare also Woods, 1987), and clamoured for government to act. Even that most doctrinaire of policy-makers, Treasury Under-Secretary Charles Trevelyan, was jolted by reports such as those just quoted for a time, and the immediate policy response was influenced by the publicity given to mass mortality.

The poor reacted vigorously at first to the crisis. Food rioting was widespread, and secret agrarian societies (locally organized but generically known as Ribbonmen) stepped up their activities (Donnelly, 1973, *187–91*).[34] Still, the full story of this popular resistance and its repression, which holds great potential for comparative insight on issues such as the moral economy and farmer–labourer conflict, remains to be told. Meanwhile the crime statistics help highlight the extent of the upsurge. They show, for example, that the number of persons committed for trial rose from an average of fewer than 20,000 in 1842–6 to 31,209 in 1847, 38,522 in 1848, and 41,989 in 1849.[35] Cross-tabulations by type of crime show that the surge was more the product of desperation than of malice: the number of committals for non-violent offences against property trebled, while that for offences against the person (homicide, wounding, and sexual offences) hardly rose at all. The

---

[33]   R. M. Hartwell (1959) 'Interpretations of the Industrial Revolution', *Journal of Economic History*, xix, 229–49.

[34]   Charles Townshend (1983) *Political Violence in Ireland: Government and Resistance since 1848* (Oxford), pp. 18–21. See too Jonathan Pim (1855–6) 'Address Delivered at the Opening of the Session of the Society', *Journal of the Dublin Statistical Society*, i, 18–19, 30–1.

[35]   Data on the number of crimes reported tell a similar story, though they peak earlier. Crimes outside the Dublin metropolitan area rose from 8,088 in 1845 to 12,380 in 1846, and peaked at 20,986 in 1847. They exceeded 14,000 in both 1848 and 1849, and then dropped off sharply. Cf. State Papers Office Dublin, Returns of Outrages 1846–55.

dramatic rise in the proportion of illiterates among those charged during the Famine (from 30 to over 40 per cent) also supports this interpretation. Striking too is the persistence of high crime rates until 1849, after which the crime rate dropped off sharply.

The mounting death toll prompted a series of policy initiatives. The then-traditional policy of providing work for the poor on public schemes through a Board of Works had been reintroduced by Peel in March 1846. This continued but with more central supervision, with Russell's Labour Rate Act. The cost of acceptable schemes was to fall 'entirely on persons possessed of property in the distressed districts'. Nevertheless, a flood of applications ensued, and for a time the Board was handling about 1,000 letters a day. The official in charge, Colonel Harry Jones, described the Board of Works in the following months as 'a great bazaar' (quoted in Griffiths, 1970). Whitehall insisted on projects combining a high social and low private value. There was a cry in Ireland for 'reproductive' works, meaning land reclamation, drainage projects, and estate improvement generally. It was held that these would directly raise farm output, but the official preference for schemes such as road works and quays won out. The skill intensity of the projects selected was necessarily low: 'the work was chosen for the people, not the people for the work'. By October 1846 hundreds of projects were already employing over 100,000 people; 20,000 of the workers lived in a single county – Clare – while the whole province of Ulster accounted for only 1,200.

The schemes were proposed by local 'presentment sessions', bodies composed of local taxpayers with ultimate responsibility for repaying the cost. A sense of desperation, coupled perhaps with the conviction that government in the end would not exact repayment in full, bred fiscal irresponsibility. There was never the slightest hope that local taxpayers could repay the cost of all the schemes proposed, or even those sanctioned by the Board of Works. By the end of 1846 the Board was already exasperated, but the number of relief works under its aegis continued to mount, and by the following spring they had cost nearly £5 million. At the peak in March 1847 a vast army of almost three-quarters of a million was employed, at less than a subsistence wage, on works which made little sense in terms of either economy or their goal of staving off famine. Partly because they were failing in their main task, partly because it was feared that they would 'crowd out' farm work, they were quickly disbanded in the spring of 1847. This policy reversal left its mark on the rural landscape; it left farmers cut off from their fields by unfinished roads, cottages isolated on cuttings, 'constant and unsightly monument(s) of a disastrous period'. Such eyesores would have been a small price to pay for staving off starvation, but the Board's low-wage policy ruled that out. In a pointed 'final report' on its relief role, the Board expressed the hope that 'labour will not in future be lowered to the purpose of relief, nor relief deprived of its character of benevolence' (Irish University Press, 'Famine series', 1968, *vol. 8, 383*).

The provision of 'soup' or gruel – in effect 'any food cooked in a boiler, and distributed in a liquid state' (O'Rourke, 1902, *427*) – under the Destitute Poor (Ireland) Act, which came into operation in March 1847, seemed a step in the right direction. It attempted to tackle the problem of subsistence directly, and was less likely than the public works to 'crowd out' other employment. The cost was supposed to come from rates and charity, supplemented *pro rata* by government aid. During the summer of 1847 millions of meals were provided by local relief committees: in July the number fed reached 3 million daily. In some places more meals were provided daily than there were people. The distribution of soup was an impressive feat, and historians rate the scheme a success. The soup kitchens have not been subjected to close analytical scrutiny, however. True, mortality fell off during the summer of 1847 but this was, in part at least, a seasonal phenomenon. Whether soup alone would have prevented the mass mortality of the following winter is a moot point, because the last of the government soup kitchens were wound up, amid protest, at the end of September 1847. In practice the food value of the often watery soup was low, and the people were routinely humiliated by being made to queue for hours. Yet this was arguably 'by far the most effective of all the methods adopted by government' (Donnelly, 1988).

The Irish Poor Law Extension Act of June 1847 switched the main burden of relief to the Irish Poor Law system. The switch was prompted by a fall in food prices and an anticipated seasonal rise in the demand for labour. The workhouses, it was believed, could now cope with the numbers requiring relief. However, the workhouse system had been devised for the quite different purpose of coping with non-crisis poverty. It could not handle the larger responsibility, and during 1848 one-quarter of all Boards of Guardians, mainly those located in the poorest areas, were dissolved by the Commissioners in Dublin. Cross-subsidization *within* Ireland through the highly unpopular 'rate-in-aid' shifted some of the burden to more prosperous unions (Woodham-Smith, 1962, *378–9*). Clearly the workhouses themselves, though they had greatly expanded their capacity, could not house all the poor. Outdoor relief was widely relied on: in July 1849 the workhouses still housed over 200,000 people, but another 800,000 were on outdoor relief. The principle of 'less eligibility' was pressed home by the infamous Gregory Clause, which barred tenants who held more than one-quarter of an acre of land from relief. But the decision, taken in the summer of 1847, to throw the burden of relief on the Irish Poor Law and the Irish taxpayer was the most cynical move of all. It amounted to a declaration that, as far as Whitehall was concerned, the Famine was over. This callous act, born of ideology and frustration, prolonged the crisis. In the west roadside deaths were still commonplace in the winter of 1848–9 (Ó Gráda, 1988, *86–8*; Woodham-Smith, 1962, *406–7*).

Unfortunately for Ireland, the height of the Famine period – late 1846 and early 1847 – was one of financial crisis in Britain. The 'railway mania' which began in 1845 had run its course, and bad harvests in both Ireland and Britain in 1846 led to a huge trade deficit and consequent drain of bullion on the Bank of England. The ensuing sharp rise in the cost of credit embarrassed many companies. The value of cotton output fell by a quarter. The financial crisis of 1847 thus had 'real' origins, though it was exacerbated (so most economists argue) by the restrictiveness of the Bank Act of 1844. The crisis was relatively short-lived, but it was one of the nineteenth century's worst, and from Ireland's point of view the timing was inauspicious. With the plight of the Bank of England to worry them, it is easier to see how Ireland's problems took a back seat in the minds of Russell and Wood.

The history of the Famine has always been handled without due attention to its short-term impact on the Irish economy. The crisis left no sector unscathed. Censal occupational data show that while agriculture was worst hit, other sectors, dependent either directly

Table 2.1 *Money in circulation in Ireland during the Famine*

Week ending	Notes of £5 and over	Notes less than £5	Total note circulation	Specie held by banks
3 Jan. 1846	3,039,855	4,364,509	7,404,366	2,489,254
2 Jan. 1847	3,151,117	4,364,295	7,515,414	2,608,012
1 Jan. 1848	2,502,756	2,693,357	5,196,116	1,618,760
27 Jan. 1849	2,303,587	2,371,148	4,674,739	1,645,463
11 Aug. 1849	2,109,704	1,723,367	3,833,072	1,687,778
10 Aug. 1850	2,128,956	1,949,296	4,078,255	1,423,349

Source: *Thom's Directory*, 1847–50.

or indirectly on purchases from farmers and labourers, suffered severely too. The numbers in Table 2.1 tell the story in another way. The dramatic and sustained falling off in monetary circulation can be explained neither by the crisis of 1847 (which it outlasted) nor by legislative reform. Its connection with the Famine is underlined by the dramatic drop in the circulation of low-denomination banknotes, used in transactions such as wage payments and the business dealings of the poor. The amount of silver specie held by the banks (Table 2.1 refers to gold specie only) also fell markedly.[36] 1846 was a boom year for business and banks, but 1847 presented difficulties as the price of corn plummeted, and rents were not paid.[37] These years saw too the creation of Ireland's rail system. Between 1845 and 1853 track mileage grew from 70 to 700 miles, and in 1846–8 railway construction projects employed on average about 40,000 men. The benefits of railway investment for the Irish economy proved more lasting than those of the roads and bridges built by a far larger army of emaciated workers on public relief. But while the long-run consequences of the network were very important, this railway boom could do little to alleviate the Famine.[38]

[36] See 'The Agricultural and Commercial Condition of Ireland: The Bank Returns (1849) *Dublin University Magazine*, 34, 372–80. These numbers are a better measure of the Famine's impact than the trend in bank deposits, which fell in 1847 but rose thereafter. Cf. Philip Ollerenshaw (1987) *Banking in Nineteenth-Century Ireland: The Belfast Banks, 1825–1914* (Manchester), pp. 70–2.

[37] F. G. Hall (1947) *The Bank of Ireland 1783–1946* (Dublin), pp. 216–24.

[38] Joseph Lee (1965) 'An Economic History of Early Irish Railways' (unpublished M.A. thesis, National University of Ireland), pp. 140–2, 170–2.

The trend of weekly deaths in the poorhouses is a fallible but still useful indication of the spread of the deaths over time. The numbers highlight the seasonality of deaths and – more importantly – the long-drawn-out character of the crisis (Mokyr and Ó Gráda, 1984, *84–6*). Now famine deaths, it is true, usually outlast the literal shortage of food, but in Ireland what shocks is the *size* of the excess mortality in 1848–50. The continuing winter mortality peaks point like accusing fingers pointed at the official determination to declare the crisis over in the summer of 1847. The precise number who died will never be known, though guesses abound (Boyle and Ó Gráda, 1986; Cousens, 1963; Mokyr, 1980b). Some recent revisionist accounts have reduced the figure to 0.5 million, but Woodham-Smith has proposed 1.5 million (1962, *411*) and the *New Encyclopedia Britannica* puts deaths as high as 2–3 million.[39] Civil registration data on mortality are lacking, but by extrapolating the censal population estimates of 1841 to 1851, and allowing for non-crisis mortality and migration, an estimate of famine mortality is generated as a residual. In practice, incomplete Famine emigration data present a problem. No proper count was kept of the *flow* to Britain: only data on the number of Irish living in Britain in 1851 are available. Nor do passenger list tabulations, the best source on the numbers who boarded ships to move further afield, capture everybody either. In calculating excess mortality it is thus easy for the historian to consign to a premature grave some who escaped abroad unnoticed. For what they are worth, two recent estimates confirm the traditional guess of an excess mortality of 1 million, or one in nine of the whole population (Mokyr, 1980b; Boyle and Ó Gráda, 1986). Both ignore the difficulties of disentangling cholera deaths from the total, and base their assumptions about 'normal' mortality on imperfect censal data. Mokyr (1980b) reminds us that the Famine also reduced the birth rate below the 'normal' level, and argues the case for including such averted births as famine victims. He puts their number at about 0.4 million.[40]

If scientific diagnosis of the potato blight was crude, medical

---

[39] Compare Mary Daly (1980) *The Economic History of Ireland since 1800* (Dublin), pp. 20–1: T. Garvin (1981) *The Evolution of Irish Nationalist Politics* (Dublin), p. 54; *Encyclopedia Britannica* (15 edn, New York, 1974), p. 674.

[40] However, as Kennedy (1983, *210*) points out, Mokyr overlooks the 'reincarnation' of some of these as the children of emigrants.

science was ineffective in preventing the ensuing deaths. Ireland had a large number of hospitals (about 40 regular and 60 fever hospitals) and over 600 dispensaries. These hospitals and dispensaries, largely the relics of earlier crises, survived on a combination of public funds and local enterprise. Worthy institutions, they were often poorly managed, and their spread was inverse to need. Medical practitioners grumbled about their rewards for famine duties. The work was dangerous, however: 36 of the 473 men appointed as medical officers by the Board of Health died of the occupational hazard of famine fever. But medical men had no remedies for fever or dysentry beyond what commonsense dictated. The treatment meted out in fever hospitals in the 1840s – deemed 'lazarettos for the reception of the sick' by Dublin's leading physician, Dominick Corrigan – was still fumigation with sulphuric acid and 'nitre', and the baking of victims' clothes.[41]

Those who died better-publicized deaths during the first famine winter in places such as Skibbereen perished of starvation, and of dysentery induced by infected and unwholesome foods. But 'no famine, no fever', and later deaths were disproportionately due to fever. Relapsing sickness, a less virulent form of fever endemic in Ireland, was accompanied by (and sometimes confused with) the more murderous typhus. Typhus was more likely to attack all socioeconomic groups, and once the rich contracted it, they were more likely to succumb than the poor. The cholera epidemic of 1849 was undoubtedly intensified by the Famine. Cholera's first visitation in 1832–3 had killed 25,000. The higher toll in 1849–50 – the 1851 census put the total at 36,000 – may be attributed in large part to the effects of the Famine, for a double reason: casualties were more frequent where the Famine was gravest and, besides, well-fed people can usually withstand or recover from cholera infection.

Who perished? The Famine presumably forced many families, like the occupants of an overloaded lifeboat, to make life-and-death choices: an equal sharing of the burden of hunger might have doomed all. Were the young sacrificed so that others might live? The admittedly curious tale of an infant 'at the mother's breast [who] had to be removed' so that its teenage brother 'might

[41] See Peter Froggatt (1987) 'The Response of the Medical Profession to the Great Famine', in (Crawford).

receive sustenance from his mother to enable him to remain at work' highlights the issue (O'Rourke, 1902, *274*). A recent study of the Famine's incidence by age and sex shows that crisis mortality was almost a straightforward multiple of ordinary mortality. Children under 10 years and old people over 60 were over-represented among the famine dead; they accounted for less than one-third of the population but three-fifths of the deaths. Thus in a sense the very old and young were 'sacrificed'. But such proportions held in normal times also (Boyle and Ó Gráda, 1986). In this the Great Famine resembled the Bengali famine of 1940–3. The pattern is by no means inevitable, however (Watkins and Menken, 1985, *654–6*); Irish famine mortality was the product of a particular combination of the 'lifeboat ethics' described above, dysentry which tended to target the young, and typhus which was more inclined to attack the elderly.

(ii) Ideology and relief

The history of the Irish Famine is also British political history. By mid-October 1845 the potato failure had convinced Peel that only 'the removal of all impediments to the import of all kinds of human food' would remove the threat of famine, and this dramatic reversal of a key Tory policy – the Corn Laws – led to his political downfall eight months later (Gash, 1972, *538*). Other leading politicians of the day, from Whig (or Liberal Party) leader Lord John Russell to Tory protectionist Lord George Bentinck, were less inclined to bend their previous views. The range of attitudes in high places towards public help for the Irish is curious. In terms of today's political alignments, the Tories of the time would be considered 'liberal'. Peel's determined action in 1845–6 has often been contrasted with the harsh policies of Russell and Wood at the height of the Famine,[42] while Bentinck was a vocal supporter of more spending in Ireland, in particular on railways. Against this,

[42] Compare the contrast in India a few decades later between two successive Governors General, one throwing 'all his resources into saving lives', the other 'trusting to the workings of the market to perform the same job'. S. Ambirajan (1976) 'Malthusian Theory and Indian Famine Policy in the Nineteenth Century', *Population Studies*, 30, 6.

Whig spokesmen such as Whately and Senior believed that preventing mass mortality was simply impossible. Even attempting to do so was wrong, since it would bankrupt Irish landlords, and the ensuing demoralization would destroy 'industry' and 'self-dependence' and ultimately put a stop to economic activity. The Whigs, too, were consistent in their faith in the market, and their text might have been Adam Smith's dictum that 'the free exercise (of trade) is not only the best palliative of the inconveniences of a dearth, but the best preventative of that calamity'.[43]

The contrast oversimplifies, for Peel as long ago as 1822 had articulated those same fears of generous relief now so emphasized by the Whigs. But he had felt and insisted too that 'the exigency of the present case precludes any consideration of ultimate results'.[44] Nor were political groupings in the 1840s as ideologically monolithic as today. Clarendon, the Whig Lord Lieutenant, was much more eager for aid than his colleagues in Whitehall. The split in the Tory ranks on the Corn Laws spilled over into Irish policy, and after his defeat in July 1846 Peel tended to support the Whig ministry against Bentinck from the backbenches. Again, some of the Whig reluctance to spend may be traced to their wish to embarrass Irish landlords, in the main supporters of the Tories. But once more the distinction is hardly clearcut, since several leading Irish landlords were influential Whigs. Yet the ideological tensions that divided Whig and Tory on the Poor Law and factory legislation are also reflected in Famine relief policy. In line with their more *noblesse oblige* attitude toward social welfare legislation, the Tories at least paid lip service to more food aid, a less restrictive use of the Poor Law, more public spending on the infrastructure, and subsidies to improving landlords.

Leading Whigs and Radicals, by contrast, insisted on the evils of public charity and the 'inevitability' of the outcome. They were strongly supported in this by the *Edinburgh Review* and the fledgling *Economist*. Avoiding deaths was not the prime Whig preoccupation: relief would shift the distribution of food 'from the more meritorious to the less', because 'if left to the natural law of

---

[43] A. Smith (1976) *An Inquiry into the Nature and Causes of the Wealth of Nations* (Oxford), p. 532. Compare P. Samuelson (1967) *Economics*, 7th edn (New York), p. 45 (quoted in Ambirajan, p. 63n).

[44] O'Neill, 'The Famine of 1822', ch. 3, p. 51

distribution, those who deserved more would obtain it'.[45] Thus in the Commons Russell refused to commit himself to saving lives as the prime objective, and some Whig ideologues such as Nassau Senior and *The Economist's* Thomas Wilson ('it is no man's business to provide for another') countenanced large-scale mortality with equanimity. In India as in Ireland, Whig logic highlighted the abuses of intervention, and made light of the cost in human lives (Ambirajan, 1978, *ch.3*). It is easy to see why populist and socialist critics saw this as Malthusian murder by the invisible hand (see Gibbon, 1975). Ironically historians have been dismissive of the likes of Bentinck and William Smith O'Brien, who showed far more humanity then either, say, Lord Brougham or John Roebuck, MP for Bath, remembered today as enlightened men. But historical wrath has been reserved for permanent Treasury Under-Secretary Charles Trevelyan, the able but arrogant mandarin responsible for day-to-day policy decisions during the Famine. Trevelyan, very much the villain in Woodham-Smith's plot (1962), has an able defender in Austin Bourke, who contrasts Trevelyan's more dogmatic pronouncements under Russell with a more flexible stance earlier under Peel.[46] With Russell in command, claims Bourke, Trevelyan's humanitarian instincts could find no voice. An analysis of Trevelyan's private papers, however, lends little support to this view. It shows that the Under-Secretary, a deeply religious man, fully believed throughout that the Famine had been ordained by God to teach the Irish a lesson, and therefore should not be too much interfered with (Hart, 1960). In India, Trevelyan's thinking on Ireland was invoked by bureaucrats in the 1850s to justify keeping interference to a minimum (Ambirajan, 1978, *79*).

The Whig belief in the power of free markets to direct food where most needed dictated a policy of *laissez-faire* in so far as supply was concerned. Demand would be met by the purchasing power of money wages earned on the public works. Tying relief to work would minimize sponging, and limiting works to infrastructural projects would leave private investment unaffected. In theory the policy thus aimed at distortion-free relief. In practice, however, relief measures taken during the worst of the crisis were

---

[45] *The Economist*, 30 January 1847.
[46] Austin Bourke (1977) 'Apologia for a Dead Civil Servant', *Irish Times*, 5–6 July.

reluctant and wrong-headed. As noted earlier, policy relied on competitive market forces to keep prices down. High prices would increase supply through either imports or reduced exports of grain. In economic jargon this amounts to no more than the hope that the market provides a Pareto-optimal outcome (*) even in famine conditions. Whether the market was powerful enough to control speculation and hoarding is difficult to say. Folklore and literary fiction stress the huge profits made by village merchant-cum-usurers, but the man in the street typically cannot distinguish between hoarding and supply-and-demand fundamentals as the cause of high prices. While some traders in remote areas no doubt prospered – even government acknowledged as much – there is no theoretical presumption that monopoly power rises in times of crisis. Hard evidence is lacking. The gombeenman or 'meal-monger', vilified in folk memory but without whom matters might have been worse still, certainly charged more during the Famine than before. But was this monopoly extortion, or a reaction to higher default rates? The unlovable gombeenmen have left few traces for the historian to assess. The evidence from the country's biggest potato market, that of Dublin, is at least consistent with no hoarding, because hoarding would have led to high prices after harvest-time, but a smaller rise in price thereafter as traders rid themselves of their hoards before they rotted in the late spring or early summer. This implies a seasonal price pattern not observed in the data (Ó Gráda, 1988, *ch. 3*). Thus it would seem that deaths were not due to the failure of the market to work. The question warrants full investigation, especially since research elsewhere points to speculative bubbles and market failure during famines.[47]

The massive mortality has understandably prompted the verdict that 'relief operations . . . made no impression on starvation' (Gibbon, 1975, *132*). None of the policies pursued was beyond criticism. The public works were a tremendous achievement in *bureaucratic* terms, and made sense to the extent that most of the money went to labourers. About 90 per cent of the outlays went on wages, and the necessarily large bureaucracy took only 7 per cent.

[47]   See e.g. Salim Rashid (1980) 'The Policy of Laissez-Faire During Scarcities', *Economic Journal*, 90, and Martin Ravallion (1987) *Markets and Famines* (Oxford).

Nor is the inevitable petty cheating and malingering, sensational-
ized by critics at the time (e.g. Senior, 1968), the issue. There were
more serious problems. First, as already noted, the outcome too
often was 'work which will answer no other purpose than that of
obstructing the public conveyances' (Woodham-Smith, 1962,
180). From October 1846 landlords were allowed to sponsor
works that would improve their properties, provided they accepted
responsibility for all the charges incurred. The conditions were too
onerous, and this measure achieved little. The maximum number
employed on estate improvement never reached more than a tiny
fraction of those on the roads. Second, payment by results on the
public works benefited those with some capital and those still
healthy, and widened the gap between these and the most needy
over time. By the end of 1846 the Board was already declaring that
the problem had become 'one of food, not labour' (Irish University
Press, 'Famine Series', 1968, *VIII, 383*), but the claim is imprecise.
What was lacking was the *purchasing power* to command subsistence at prevailing prices. On average, the Board paid its workers
about 12d. *per diem*, enough for a family to subsist on in normal
times, but now literally a starvation wage (Irish University Press,
'Famine Series', 1968, *VI, 190–1*; *VII, 537*). Third, money spent
on the works did not always necessarily reflect famine conditions,
because the local organization necessary to request schemes seems
to have been lacking in some of the worst blackspots. The cost of
the projects constructed by starving workers was high, of course. In
south-west Cork in 1845 the regular presentment sessions were
allowing 12 shillings per perch for roads; by the end of the
following year, the cost was over £2, stark evidence of both
enforcement problems and the declining strength of workers.[48]

Another key element of policy, local responsibility, told most
against those areas least equipped to fend for themselves. Thus
though thousands were starving in west Cork in December 1846,
even there the '*main point*' was to get local subscriptions, since
'there must be somebody . . . capable of some contribution'.
Matching grants represented a peculiarly regressive form of gov-
ernmental assistance (Irish University Press, 'Famine Series',
1962, *5, 849*).

---

[48] Hickey, *op. cit.*, p. 356.

The public works may have provided the framework, but they failed to provide the funds for preventing starvation. Mass emigration, properly subsidized and regulated, would also have reduced mortality. Instead, the government relied largely on unaided individual effort. To a widely-supported scheme of assisted emigration to Canada proposed in the spring of 1847, Russell's riposte was dismissive (O'Rourke, 1902, *493–6*). Of course, the crisis produced a massive exodus regardless: between 1845 and 1855 about 1.5 million left for good, double the numbers that would have left otherwise. Emigration in 1845 was unaffected by the blight. Next year's blight did not strike until the usual passage season was almost over, yet over 100,000 left for North America, the highest in any year until then. But 1847 produced an exodus of one-quarter of a million, and an average outflow of 200,000 or more was recorded for the next five years. Then the numbers fell and were down to about 70,000 by 1855. Most of this migration was unaided by other than family members, often through emigrant remittances. Recent calculations imply that no more than 3 or 4 per cent had their passages paid by landlord or government, though others were subsidized by charity and rent rebates (Fitzpatrick, 1984; Edwards and Williams, 1956, *ch. 6*). Most of the migrants ended up in the United States.

Not surprisingly, the Famine migration differed from earlier movements in several respects (Fitzpatrick; Miller, 1985; MacDonagh in Edwards and Williams, 1956). First the poor were better represented, though the very poorest were more likely to succumb to the Famine at home than to emigrate. Second, it was more likely to consist of family groupings than either earlier or later movements. Third, the regional composition of the Famine exodus was different too. As noted earlier, migration before 1845 tended to be from the richer provinces of Leinster and Ulster, but the Famine gave the spur to mass migration from the poorer west and south-west, establishing a trend that has lasted till this day. Fourth, the migration of 1847 exacted a higher toll in lives *en route* than earlier crossings. In theory the emigrant was protected from corrupt agents and shipowners by the Passenger Acts, but the machinery and personnel in place for enforcing existing controls were completely inadequate. The screening of passengers already stricken with fever was inadequate, and overcrowding and the lack of proper food and medical care led to more. Mortality on the Atlantic passage in 1847, particularly on the Canadian route, was high (Mokyr, 1983, *267–8*; MacDonagh in Edwards and Williams, 1956; McDonagh, 1961). The emigration commissioners charged with protecting passengers from abuse reacted timorously, 'oppressed by a sense of general Treasury disapproval'. Legislation could not have eliminated all abuses without placing the traffic as a whole at risk. Some emigrants were bound to perish: the supply of proper ships and medical inspectors was too inelastic in the short run to cope. Yet here too dogmatism cost lives, before the existing legislation was tightened up and acted upon. The outcome was a retreat from laissez-faire and free contract (McDonagh, 1961).[49]

The sums spent on relief by government are on record. In 1850 the Treasury put its outlay since 1845 at just over £8 million. The remission of public works loans and the soup kitchens accounted for less than half of this; the rest was in the form of loans which had not been repaid by 1850. These were consolidated then, and written off in 1853. Ireland spent more than this on famine relief. The poor rates produced over £7 million, while landlords spent an unknown amount privately, and borrowed over a million (Donnelly, 1989). Historians disagree about the significance of the sums spent by government. The tone of Edwards and Williams (1956, *vii–xvi*) is distinctly apologetic; awestruck by the '[impressive] extent of the actual outlay', they urge that to expect more is anachronistic. However, they chose to ignore those contemporary critics who repeatedly protested at the stinginess of aid. Complaints that 'England could find a hundred millions of money to spend in fighting the Grand Turk', 20 millions to compensate West Indian slave-owners for freeing their slaves, or a similar sum for 'the luxury of shooting King Theodore', while funds could not be found to save Irish lives, were commonplace (O'Rourke, 1902, *162*; Ó Gráda, 1988, *ch. 3*). A curious feature of the literature is that non-Irish Famine specialists are less inhibited than Irish historians in their critiques of policy. Thus Mokyr (1983, *291–2*) and Donnelly (1988) stress the limitations of relief policy. And, relative to output or total

---

[49] See too Philip Taylor (1972) *The Distant Magnet: European Migration to the U.S.A.* (London), pp. 107–16.

government spending, spending on Irish famine relief indeed seems small. Spread out over the period of the Famine, outlays were about 0.3 per cent of GNP or 2-3 per cent of public expenditure. Total gross public liabilities were *less* after the Famine than before it. Such arithmetic exaggerates the impact of relief, since much of the generosity was *ex post*. Had this been fully grasped before, spending might have been geared more towards helping the most needy. Like the British standard-of-living debate, positions on the Great Famine tend to reflect political biases. Thus it is hardly surprising, however depressing, to find the eminent historian John Clapham claiming 'that the indiscriminate provision of relief . . . was still further directing the Irish from the steady industry and increased self-help which alone, in the end, could save them', or Ireland's leading Marxist thinker insisting instead 'that England made the Famine by a rigid application of the economic principles that lie at the base of capitalist society'.[50]

Private generosity helped, but was unequal to the problem (Woodham-Smith, 1962, *382–3*). The generosity of some groups, including the much-publicized efforts of the Society of Friends, was matched by those who raised funds, largely under Catholic auspices, in America and Australia. Emigrant remittances flowed in too (Miller, 1985). Nearer home, however, private charity was in short supply during the Great Famine. English charity had been crucial in 1822 and 1831. What changed in the interim? Several possible reasons have been outlined by Tim O'Neill. The passing of the Irish Poor Law in 1838 may have crowded out some private charity, and the feeling in middle-class Britain that Irish property was reneging on its responsibilities was encouraged by ministers and the press. But exaggerated perceptions of Irish criminality, anti-Catholic bigotry, and British disillusionment with agitator-parliamentarian Daniel O'Connell and his campaign for the Repeal of the Union, all played a role (see Senior, 1868).[51] Finally, 'donor fatigue' is indicated by the ebbing of private charity in 1848 and later.

---

[50] J. H. Clapham (1943) 'A Source for the Historian', in *The Economist 1843–1943: A Centenary Volume* (Oxford), p. 39; James Connolly, quoted in (Gibbon, 1975).

[51] T. O'Neill, 'The State, Poverty and Distress', pp. 304–6.

(iii) Regional dimensions

Another important aspect of the crisis is its regional dimension. The numbers on the public works highlight this. In mid-March 1847 in Connacht there was an average of one individual per family on the works; in the least affected counties (Dublin and eastern Ulster) the ratio was one man per sixteen families. The death toll was highly uneven regionally. The Famine killed few in the north-east and there it was soon over. Cemetery returns suggest some excess mortality in Dublin, where the crisis prompted a massive inflow of beggars and vagrants. But the cholera outbreak of 1849 seems to have killed more in the capital than famine fever or starvation. Even in some poor but less potato-dependent parts of Ulster the decline was small: in the west Donegal parish of Tulloghobegley,[52] population fell modestly, from 9,049 in 1841 to 8,982 in 1851. In the prosperous Wexford baronies of Forth and Bargy, where population growth had been moderate before the Famine, numbers hardly fell at all. The provinces of Munster and Connacht, with less than half the population of Ireland in 1841, accounted for well over two-thirds of the excess deaths, and Connacht's population decline was almost double that of Leinster. Still, misery was widely diffused and only one county of the 32 (Dublin) increased its population between 1841 and 1851. The occupational data in the census reports of 1841 and 1851 also highlight the differential regional impact of the Famine: Table 2.2, with summary data for the badly-hit province of Connacht and the south-eastern county Wexford, captures the range. Wexford escaped lightly, but *all* sectors of Connacht's population were hit (compare Kennedy and Ollerenshaw, 1985, *25–30*.

The lack of Irish research on the Famine is well reflected in the paucity of regional studies. The south-west has been relatively well served. Donnelly (1973) focuses on the rural economy of Cork during the crisis, while Patrick Hickey's account of part of the same county, the severely-hit area around Schull and

---

[52] Lord George Hill's widely-read *Facts from Gweedore* (London, 1846) provides a bleak description of the area.

Table 2.2 *Occupation distribution in Wexford and Connacht 1841–1851 (males aged 15+, in thousands) (percentages in brackets)*

Sector	Connacht		Wexford	
	1841	1851	1841	1851
Food	324 (84.8)	220 (83.7)	42 (73.7)	38 (74.5)
Clothing	21 (5.5)	11 (4.2)	4 (7.0)	3 (5.9)
Lodging	16 (4.2)	12 (4.6)	5 (8.8)	4 (7.8)
Other	21 (5.5)	20 (7.6)	6 (10.5)	6 (11.8)
Total	382	263	57	51

Source: 1841 and 1851 Census Reports.

Skibereen,[53] is the only scholarly work of its kind so far and confirms the popular impression – based on the great publicity given to hardship in the area by the *Illustrated London News* and press reports – that the crisis was worst there. Perhaps further such studies will show that other western counties, such as Clare, Kerry and Mayo, suffered equally, but in silence (O'Rourke, 1902, *268–9, 383*). Yet even in the south and west there are areas where allegedly the Famine did little damage. Scholarly accounts of the Famine at local level are almost nonexistent. Parish and local histories are plentiful, but they lack comparative perspective, and are usually based on linking secondary sources such as Woodham-Smith (1962) and Edwards and Williams (1956) to local primary sources such as contemporary newspapers, and perhaps the Poor Law Guardians' and relief commissioners' reports.[54]

Much could be learned from local studies about the efficacy of different relief policies, the role of landlords, commercialization, and topography. The history of the Aran islands off the Galway and Clare coasts, with a population of over 3,000 souls in 1841, is a tantalizing case in point. Its poverty and remoteness made Aran

[53] 'A Study of Four Peninsular Parishes'. Also worth noting, Kieran Foley's (1987) 'The Killarney Poor Law Guardians and the Famine 1845–52' (unpublished M.A. thesis, National University of Ireland).

[54] Good examples include Edward Garner (1986) *To Die By Inches: The Famine in North-east Cork* (Cork); Sean Kierse (1984) *The Famine Years in the Parish of Killaloe 1845–1851* (Killaloe); A. T. Culloty (1986) *Ballydesmond/Baile Deasmhumhan: A Rural Parish in its Historical Setting* (Dublin), ch. 6; Ned McHugh (1986) 'Famine and Distress in Drogheda During 1847', *Journal of the County Louth Archaeological and Historical Society*, XXI (2).

at least as likely a candidate for Malthusian retribution as any part of the country, but both folkmemory and the statistical record suggest that it escaped the Famine's ravages lightly. Whether this was because it was partially spared the blight, or because fish was plentiful during the crisis, is not clear, but Aran relied little on relief during the Famine years, and its population declined but little. If indeed Aran pulled through as indicated, it offers a glimpse at that might-have-been, an Ireland spared the blight in the 1840s. In the long run the islands' population dropped as elsewhere, but at a lower cost in terms of human suffering (Ó Gráda, 1988, *ch. 3*).

Nowhere else in Europe did the potato's failure exact as high a price as in Ireland. Yet the ensuing misery in Scotland's Highlands and in parts of Germany was considerable, while in the Netherlands and in Belgium (where the potato was much less central to the diet than in Ireland) the blight also led to significant mortality. Mokyr has put excess deaths in the Netherlands at about 60,000 (or one-fifth the Irish rate), but in Flanders, where a severe crisis in the linen industry compounded the difficulties, the toll was about 50,000 in a population of only 1.4 million.[55]

(iv) Food entitlements (*)

A pivotal sound in Irish playwright Thomas Murphy's rendition of the Famine tragedy is 'the noise of a convoy of corn-carts on a road'.[56] This evokes the enduring populist lament that the fundamental problem in 1846 and after was not the availability of food, but grain being shipped out of Ireland to pay rents as the people starved. If food was scarce why not balance supply and demand at a lower price by halting grain exports? Government relied instead on the self-correcting power of the price mechanism and free trade to match supply and demand, pinning their hopes on a quick supply response from overseas. They had the authority of Adam Smith and Edmund Burke on their side in rejecting any inter-

---

[55] Joel Mokyr (1980) 'Industrialization and Poverty in Ireland and Netherlands', *Journal of Interdisciplinary History*, x (3), 436–7; Flinn *et al.*, *op. cit.*, pp. 430–8.
[56] T. Murphy (1977) *Famine* (Dublin), p. 23.

Table 2.3 *Grain exports and imports 1844–8 (in thousands of tons)*

	Exports	Imports	Net movement
1844	424	30	+394
1845	513	28	+485
1846	284	197	+87
1847	146	889	−743
1848	314	439	−125

Source: (Bourke, 1976).

ference.[57] In the long run, freeing imports made more sense than prohibiting exports. And, to a point, supply response worked as indicated. By the summer of 1847, Irish markets were flooded with foreign corn and maize. In a sense the traditional populist focus on outward shipments of grain is wide of the mark because (as Table 2.3 makes clear) there was a huge drop in net exports in the late 1840s. Nevertheless, as Donnelly and others have argued, a *temporary* surprise embargo on grain exports in late 1846, in anticipation of imports already on their way, might well have helped.

Did the country produce enough food in the late 1840s to feed everybody? The puzzle evokes the typology of famine recently formalized by Sen (1981). Sen's study of modern famines suggests that the lack of food, in the literal sense of there not being enough to fill all stomachs, often fails to explain starvation. Such famines are 'artificial', the outcome of politics, speculation, or panic. The claim was not new in Ireland in 1846: both the crises of 1816–19 and 1822 had been put down to unemployment and distributional shifts rather than lack of food (Ó Gráda, 1988, *ch.* 3). But surely in 1846, when the shortfall in potatoes was massive, and the acreage under grain also fell, this was irrelevant?

An answer requires some dietary arithmetic. Let us accept Arthur Young's claim that an acre under potatoes provided enough food in an average year to feed four people, while it took twice as much land to produce the same food value in wheat. The claim is borne out by later assessments; in Britain during the First

[57] A. Smith (1976) *An Inquiry into the Nature and Causes of the Wealth of Nations* (Oxford), pp. 532–6; E. Burke (1852) 'Thoughts and Details on Scarcity. Originally presented to the Right Hon. William Pitt, in the Month of November 1795', in *The Works and Correspondence of the Right Honourable Edmund Burke* (1852), vol. v, pp. 179–212.

World War nutritionists calculated that an acre of land could feed 2.08 people on wheat or 4.18 people on potatoes (see too Mokyr and Ó Gráda, 1984, *108*). If the potato's advantage was about two to one, then about 3 million extra acres of grain would have been needed annually to meet the food shortfall caused by the blight. This was out of the question, and in this sense Sen's critique of the 'food availability doctrine' rings false for the Great Famine (see Solar, 1989). Superficially, however, it receives some support from another piece of arithmetic: if half an acre of grain was enough for subsistence, then the acreage actually under grain during the crisis, appropriately divided up, would have provided enough to feed everybody. But the underlying calculations overlook some awkward dynamics. The output consequences of redistribution cannot be assumed away, nor should feed and animal input needs be ignored.

An analysis of the Famine in a United Kingdom context provides a more plausible defence of Sen's model, although the focus of attention needs is shifted to relief once again. Had the poor in Ireland been granted a living wage on the public works during the winter of 1846–7, then no doubt an adequate supply of food would have been forthcoming from across the Irish Sea or further afield.

There is another sense, though, in which the Sen model is inappropriate to the Irish context. The pure Sen model in which 'adventitious' effects – the phrase is Louise Tilly's[58] – such as war or commercial speculation produce famine conditions, may be interpreted as a zero-sum game. Since there is enough food, there are gainers and losers. However, it is difficult to pinpoint many gainers from the Irish Famine. At the top of the socioeconomic scale, landlords found their rents shrinking, and many of them lost their estates: about one-seventh of the landed area changed hands in the wake of the crisis (Lee, 1973, *37*). At the bottom, the poor starved. In-between farmers relying on agricultural labour found that the efficiency wage – the wage which minimized the cost to them of effective hours worked – that they faced had risen. During the Famine workers were prepared to work for a bare subsistence, but that represented a rise in what farmers must pay, and many

[58] L. Tilly (1982) 'Food Entitlement, Famine and Conflict', *Journal of Interdisciplinary History*, XIV, 333–49.

must have found it not worthwhile to supply the wages. The result was an unemployment which dogmatists such as Nassau Senior put down to laziness (Senior, 1868). Only farmers who specialized heavily in livestock production – and they were still few in the 1840s – benefited from the Famine. Little affected by the rise in wages, they took full advantage of the fall in rents.

Landlords responded variously to the fall in their incomes. If traditionalist nationalist historiography underestimated the difficulties facing landlords, the evidence bears out its story of mass clearances in the wake of the potato failure. Comprehensive data are unavailable for 1847 and 1848, but between 1849 and 1854 alone proprietors evicted one-quarter of a million people, and that excludes those who 'surrendered' possession for a workhouse ticket or subsidized emigration (Donnelly, 1989). Landlord insolvency had been a problem before the Famine: in 1845 the Court of Chancery was handling estates worth £0.8 million. Indebtedness increased massively during the Famine. The Encumbered Estates Court established in 1849 was envisaged as a means of replacing the traditional penniless, thriftless landlords and middlemen by a new breed of improving landlord, possibly foreign (Black, 1960, *32–41*; Donnelly, 1973, *131*). The estates sold off by the Court in its first few years fetched rock-bottom prices. In Connacht land could be had for as little as 5 to 6 shillings per acre in 1850–2, but by 1857–8 the price had doubled.[59] The early 'bargains' were associated with fears – groundless as it turned out – of heavy and lasting outlays on paupers and rates. But the speculators who took advantage of the cheap land were not the entrepreneurs hoped for by Peel or agronomist James Caird; they were mainly members of the old landed and professional elites with money left to spend.

---

[59] Calculated from data in P. G. Lane (1969) 'The Social Impact of the Encumbered Estates Court on Counties Galway and Mayo, 1849–1858' (M.A. thesis, National University of Ireland).

3

Aftermath: Ireland after 1850

Like the Bolshevik Revolution in Russian history or the Great War in British, the Famine is the great divide in modern Irish economic and social history. Traditional historiography emphasized this watershed aspect: the Famine marked the end of 'prehistoric times in Ireland', and there followed a reaction by the people against everything linked to the pre-Famine era. An eminent folklorist's list of forsaken hallmarks ranges from wild fruit to early marriage, and from goats and donkeys to clustered human settlements (or *clachans*). More prosaically, pre-Famine Ireland has been associated with high population growth, low mobility, endemic violence, immiseration, high nuptiality; the Famine is supposed to have turned all this upside down. Yet it is now fashionable to stress the elements of continuity between pre- and post-Famine eras. According to Cullen, 'the Famine was less a national disaster than a regional and social one . . . even if a famine had not interfered, a decline in population was inevitable'. The shift from tillage to cattle, long associated with post-Famine clearances and population loss, has been extended back to the 1810s by Crotty (1966, *ch.* 2), the decline in population to the early 1840s by Carney (1977). Even the correlation between Famine-induced population decline and the disappearance of *clachans* has been disputed.[60] But perhaps this part of the recent trend to de-sensationalize the Famine has been overdone. In so far as economic and social

[60] E. E. Evans (1957) *Irish Folk Ways* (London), pp. 10–11; L. M. Cullen (1972) *An Economic History of Ireland since 1660* (London), p. 132; F. J. Carney (1975) 'Pre-Famine Irish Population: The Evidence from the Trinity College estates', *IESH*, 2; M. E. Cawley (1982–3) 'Aspects of Continuity and Change in Nineteenth-Century Rural Settlement Patterns: Findings from County Roscommon', *Studia Hibernica*, 22–3.

history can be divided into stages or epochs at all, the Famine is a dividing line. Recent estimates of agricultural output show that the shift to pasture cannot have proceeded far by 1845, and while (as we have seen) population growth was already modest throughout much of Ireland before the Famine, the claim that it had turned around is based on poor data (Lee, 1981).

In the wake of the Famine, the official view was that the price was worth paying. The assessment of the 1851 census commissioners was that 'we have every reason for thankfulness that years of suffering have been followed by years of prosperity' (Report, p. xvi), a sentiment echoed by Nassau Senior, who on a visit in 1852 saw 'neither poverty nor overpopulation' (Senior, 1868, *12*). In one crucial sense the Famine seemed indeed to 'work'. Henceforth even in the poorest areas, what was now called 'congestion' was a far cry from the overpopulation of the pre-Famine era. If previous subsistence crises had made little impact on Ireland's demographic regime, the Great Famine did so emphatically. Not only was population cut back, there was little tendency for a subsequent rise to fill the vacuum (compare Watkins and Menken, 1985). Census occupational data (see Table 3.1) show that while the farming proletariat suffered most, there was a trickle-down effect to most sectors of the economy. The most important outcome was that a rise in average living standards came with the big drop in numbers. The change is reflected in housing quality. Just before the Famine about one-third of the entire population lived in 'fourth-class' dwellings (the census commissioners' term for 'mud cabins having only one room'). By 1851 the proportion had fallen to slightly over one-tenth. The real wages of farm labourers rose (though by less than contemporary optimists claimed) as their numbers plummeted. Other less direct indices such as the rise in literacy, travel and personal savings also suggest higher living standards.

Yet Panglossian optimism is hardly warranted, for the Famine and ensuing depopulation undoubtedly had some negative consequences too. Paradoxically, it may well have reduced the average living standard of those survivors who remained in Ireland. Simple economic theory suggests that the losses to landlords may have exceeded the gains to surviving labourers and farmers. The reason for this is that those who perished were mostly landless: their incomes reflected labour's contribution at the margin, but workers

Table 3.1 *Occupations, 1841 and 1851 (in thousands) (males aged fifteen and over)*

	1841	1851
Food production and distribution	1,643	1,270
Of whom: Farmers	453	384
Farm labourers	1,133	811
Clothing	213	165
Lodging, furniture, machinery	158	137
Health, charity, justice	24	31
Education, religion	17	17
Unclassified	158	179
Total	2,213	1,799

away from the margin had been adding more to aggregate output than the marginal worker.[61] The continuing losses in the 1850s and after from blight-reduced potato yields should not be forgotten either. Linked to the Famine but fundamentally due to the demographic adjustment that would have taken place in any case, are the potential genetic effects of in-breeding in areas of drastic depopulation. These effects are only beginning to be identified and measured (Bittles *et al.* (1986) *Annals of Human Biology*, 473–87).

(i) Post-Famine famines?

Phytophthera infestans increased the year-to-year variance in potato yields after the Famine (Solar, 1989). Between 1850 and 1900 the national average yield fell below 3 tons per acre thirteen times. Poor harvests brought severe hardship, but few died. This was not least because public relief was unstinting by earlier standards. Between 1879 and 1884, for instance, ministers spent £2.6 million on a crisis that was minor compared to that of 1845–9. Though the sharp jump in the numbers relieved in Irish workhouses – 1.1 million in 1874–8, almost 1.7 million in 1879–83 – reflects acute distress, the rise in workhouse deaths (55,554 to 62,277) was not commensurate. The civil register, while incomplete, indicates that

[61] R. A. Berry and R. Soligo (1969) 'Some Welfare Aspects of International Migration', *Journal of Political Economy*, 77, 778–94.

no area was hit by literal starvation in 1879 and after. During the 1880s the combined death toll from relapsing fever and starvation was only a few dozen.[62] Also important, the workhouse test was never again applied in time of crisis. In mid-February 1880 government agreed to authorize relief for all destitute persons, whether landholders or not, marking an end to the infamous Gregory Clause. Again in 1890–2, £0.2 million was spent on public works. At their peak the works employed 16,000 people in areas whose total population hardly exceeded 100,000. Another £0.3 million was spent on seed loans, in an effort to wean cultivators away from the delicious but increasingly blight-prone 'Champion' variety. Public works became the norm: 'not a year passes', complained Irish Chief Secretary Arthur Balfour, 'without frantic appeals . . . to start relief works'. Further grants and loans were provided in 1897–8 and 1904–5, though – in an effort to control abuse – on slightly less generous grounds. The history of these aftershocks, all due to potato failure and confined to pockets in the far west, is only now being written (T. O'Neill, 1987). But none qualifies as 'famine' in the strict sense of significant excess mortality over a wide area.

Of special interest is the 'non-famine' of 1859–64. The detailed agricultural statistics for the period tell a tale of unrelieved gloom: indeed they tricked Karl Marx into producing an unduly bleak account of post-famine trends generally in *Das Kapital*.[63] The potato crop was less than two-thirds its post-famine average in 1860–2, and by mid-1863 farmers had £26 million wiped off the value of their output by a combination of crop failures, a fall in livestock numbers, and low prices. Dairy farmers particularly were in a bad way. But neither famine nor disease resulted, and numbers entering the workhouse were hardly affected. Donnelly has pointed to the role of increasing commercialization and the availability of credit (Donnelly, 1976). Censal data do indeed hint at a minor commercial revolution after the Famine; in the western province of Connacht, the number of grocers, victuallers, and kindred tradesmen per thousand population rose from about 1.0 in

---

62 Annual Report of the Local Government Board 1895, p. 49; H.C. 1894 xxv, 'Supplement to the 27th Report of the Registrar General . . . Containing Decennial Summaries . . . for 1881–1890', p. 26.
63 Karl Marx (1976) *Capital: Volume 1*, trans. Ben Fowkes (Harmondsworth), pp. 854–70.

1841 to 1.4 in 1861. But far more important was the population thinning done by the Great Famine: according to Fitzpatrick's calculations, the number of male agricultural labourers had dropped from 1.2 million or so in 1845, to 0.9 million in 1851, and 0.7 million in 1861.[64]

Ironically, some areas attempted to cling to vestiges of pre-Famine life. In parts of the west seasonal migration to England and Scotland seems to have increased for a time, keeping smallholdings viable, and restraining the drop in population. In such places the potato, though debilitated by blight, remained a firm favourite. County Mayo, for example, in the 1860s produced about 300,000 tons of potatoes annually, enough after deductions for pigs and seed to leave every man, woman and child three-quarters of a ton. While this marked a drop from the pre-Famine norm, it still represents great faith in the potato. In some remote areas population *rose* in the 1850s and 1860s, and (if census estimates are to be credited) in three parishes in the Mayo barony of Costello population was higher in 1861 than in 1841. And yet right from the Famine on – the contrast with the pre-Famine era here is crucial – the emigration rate was greatest from the south and west. Emigration thus tended to reduce regional income inequalities, though it could not wipe them out.

(ii) Population decline

The Famine triggered off a population decline that lasted in Ireland as a whole until the 1900s, and in many rural areas until this day (Table 3.2). This is often seen as the Famine's most important legacy. The Famine certainly provided the spur, but the *persistence* of population decline is perhaps better explained as the consequence of how low living standards were in Ireland in either 1800 or 1850. Here neighbouring Scotland provides a useful analogy. Though its aggregate population grew, the population of its Highland counties peaked in the mid-1840s, and continued to decline for a century, while numbers in its far northern counties fell by over one-third between 1861 and the

[64] D. Fitzpatrick (1980) 'The Disappearance of the Irish Agricultural Labourer, 1841–1912', *Irish Economic and Social History*, VII.

Table 3.2 *Population change (per cent) 1841–1961*

	1841–51	1851–81	1881–1911	1911–61	1961–81
Leinster	−15	−24	−9	+15	+34
Munster	−22	−28	−22	−18	+18
Connacht	−29	−19	−26	−31	+6
Ulster (pt.)	−23	−23	−24	−34	+6
N. Ireland	−13	−10	−4	+14	+10
Total	−20	−21	−15	0	+18

1940s.[65] In both Ireland and these poor Scottish regions the post-1845 exodus was due to the 'pull' of outside forces in the sense that it persisted despite rising living standards at home. Once started, however, it sparked off both a rise in expectations and a stock of expatriates which made it self-generating. The big rise in the proportion of never-marrieds after the Famine is perhaps best explained in the same way: if nuptiality is affected by economic forces, then it is perhaps better explained in terms of income comparisons across an ever-wider space than simply change in Ireland itself over time. Before the Famine the relative income of a marriageable Irishman was defined with reference to life in a few parishes; later the comparison embraced conditions in London or San Francisco.

The Famine meant that emigration peaked earlier in Ireland than in other countries participating in the great trans-Atlantic diaspora. The Irish outflow was so great – removing one-third to one-half of each rising generation – that it provoked repeated warnings of depopulation. Yet a blip in the 1880s apart, the Irish emigration rate declined more or less steadily in the post-Famine century, and the proportion of those born in Ireland living abroad had peaked by the turn of the century (compare Fitzpatrick, 1984, 4).

(iii) Agricultural adjustment

The immediate impact of the Famine on agriculture was to obliterate over 200,000 smallholdings and drastically to reduce the

---

[65] Flinn *et al.*, *op. cit.*, pp. 304–5.

acreage under the plough and the spade. Bourke's crop acreage estimates for 1845, together with official statistics for 1847 and 1849, tell the story. At first sight, the outcome suggests a perfect example of the Rybczynski theorem of two-sector international trade theory. This theorem predicts that a reduction in the endowment of a factor (in the case at hand, labour) will reduce by a greater than proportionate amount the output of the good intensive in that factor (tillage) and will increase the output of the other good (pastoral produce). But here, as usually in history, several things were happening at once. Post-Famine price movements also, quite independently, dictated less grain and more beef. The enduring character of the potato blight was another crucial element in the switch to pasture. Unlike calamities such as the Black Death which attacked people but left other inputs largely intact, the new fungus effectively also reduced the productive capacity of the soil in the longer run. Its impact on potato yields is difficult to separate from that of lower labour input. However, *Phytophthera* seems to have been largely responsible for continuing depressed yields. Before the Famine potato yields averaged 6 or 7 tons an acre. There is some doubt about the quality of early post-Famine yield data, but over the 1856–80 period, the average was drastically down – to only 3.2 tons. The use of copper sulphate solution, already widespread by 1900 and universal by 1914, did not quite restore earlier yields: on the eve of the Great War the average was still short of 5 tons. Lower labour intensity was presumably a factor, since many more potato-growers were now content with horse and plough rather than spade, and with less generous doses of fertilizer. The switch in potato varieties may also count for something here: perhaps the tastier and more blight-resistant varieties favoured by a wealthier post-Famine peasantry could not match the 'lumper' and its likes for yield? In any case, the reduced attraction of the blight-stricken potato reduced the advantages of tillage generally. Overall the decline in tillage was substantial and sustained (see Table 3.3). By 1876 the acreage under potatoes and grain had fallen to 2.7 million acres, by 1913 it was down to 1.8 million. Relative trends in the price of arable and livestock produce reinforced the effect of the blight and the shift in relative input prices.

Table 3.3 *Acreage under crops 1845–76 (in 1000 acres)*

Year	Potatoes	Wheat	Barley	Oats
1845	2.1	0.7	0.3	2.5
1846	0.28	0.74	0.33	2.2
1847	0.74	0.69	0.35	2.06
1876	0.88	0.12	0.22	1.49
1913	0.58	0.03	0.17	1.05

(iv) Social and political consequences

According to Woodham-Smith 'the famine left hatred behind. Between Ireland and England the memory of what was done and endured has lain like a sword' (Woodham-Smith, 1962, *412*). This is true in the sense that it was widely felt in Ireland that a more humane government could have alleviated the suffering. At its height, the Famine brought political factions together: the 'great meeting of Irish peers, members of parliament, and landlords', united in the Dublin Rotunda on 14 January 1847 to plead for help from Whitehall, was unique in Irish history. But the impact on Irish popular politics in the short run was not radicalization nor resistance, but resignation and despair. The Famine put an end to the mobilization of the Catholic middle class by O'Connell's Repeal movement; and the Young Ireland 'revolution' of July 1848, led by the inoffensive William Smith O'Brien, was a farce. In 1848, the Famine was a weak argument for national self-reliance, since no Irish administration, however sympathetic, could have handled the crisis unaided. The Famine thus brought home the irrelevance of economic nationalism.[66] In the wake of the crisis, localism was the dominant trend in politics, with the emphasis on 'drains and cash' rather than 'Repeal and reform' (Hoppen, 1984, *479*). And yet among Fenian radicals – a major force in the 1860s – the remembered wrongs of the Famine years were linked to the political demand for sovereignty. In America, too, it did not take

---

[66] 'Ireland was in their hands', Daniel O'Connell pleaded with fellow-MPs in Westminster, 'if they did not save her, she could not save herself'. (Hansard, 3rd series, vol. 89, p. 945.)

long to translate Famine memories into support for nationalism (Miller, 1985).

According to the results of the latest research, the Famine also changed the character of Irish agrarian agitation, though it must be admitted that the extent and the target of pre-Famine rural violence are still controversial issues. The traditional populist tendency to view it all as an unending battle of tenant against landlord has given way to interpretations that emphasize the tensions between farm labourers and their bosses about conacre and wages, and indeed between the tenants themselves. This new complexity does not take away from the characterization of pre-Famine agrarian agitation as local and reactive. The demise of landless labourers changed the focus of the agitation, and the rise in living standards its organization. The change is well captured in the rousing Land League slogan of summer 1880, 'Hold the harvest', a slogan which would have offered little comfort to the poor of 1847 or 1848.[67]

Earlier historians usually painted a very bleak picture of social life in Ireland after the Famine. Pre-Famine Ireland, by contrast, seemed a gregarious and cheerful place, where family ties extended far and people were neighbourly, where puritanical scruples counted for little, and where peasant life was rudely egalitarian. Some historians have argued that the crisis put an end to such features of pre-Famine life, others that such images exaggerate the Famine's role. A good example is the Lynch–Vaizey assertion that the 'extended family', along with its nefarious consequences for business enterprise, was a prime casualty of the Famine (Lynch and Vaizey, 1960, *164*). Frank Carney's research on pre-Famine household size refutes this, showing that while Irish households were typically larger than English before 1845, the difference was not due to stronger kinship ties but to higher fertility (Carney, 1977).

The Famine's part in producing a change in religiosity is also in dispute. Today Catholic Ireland remains a bastion of Mother

---

[67] The literature on rural unrest is substantial and of high quality. See especially S. Clark (1979) *The Social Origins of the Land War* (Princeton); D. Fitzpatrick (1982) 'Class, Family, and Rural Unrest in Nineteenth-century Ireland' in P. J. Drudy (ed.), *Ireland: Land, Politics, and People* (Cambridge), pp. 37–75; S. Clark and J. Donnelly (eds) (1983) *Irish Peasants: Violence and Political Unrest 1780–1914* (Wisconsin).

Church, but before the Famine, if Sunday attendance be an index, practice was lax outside the towns and the English-speaking east. Probably not more than half the country's professed Catholics attended mass regularly. Larkin has argued that, both socially and psychologically, the Famine promoted a 'devotional revolution'; socially, because the 'respectable' classes who had rallied to the cause before 1845 were relatively more dominant, and psychologically because the Famine had resulted in mass guilt and alienation conducive towards a religious revival (Larkin, 1972). Here again, though, the role of the Famine has been exaggerated. Critics of Larkin have drawn attention to the extensive church-building and to the priestly victories over traditional popular culture of the pre-Famine era (Connolly, 1985). Nor does the lax support of Famine emigrants for the Church in their seedy New World slums prove much about their religiosity at home.

The evolution of the Irish system of impartible land inheritance and its associated arranged marriages (called 'matches') has also been attributed to the Famine (Arensberg and Kimball, 1965; Connell, 1968). Connell has highlighted the contrast between the earlier co-existence of subdivision and the 'haphazard, happy-go-lucky marriages of the eighteenth and early nineteenth centuries', and the dour post-Famine regime of impartible inheritance and bridal dowries. According to Connell, the Famine taught the marriage-prone Irish a lesson, but the new preventive check mechanism had its price. It guaranteed the integrity of the family holding only at the cost of greater intra-familial inequality. The tensions caused by these arrangements have been highlighted in Irish plays and novels, but a somewhat less conflictual interpretation of the outcome is suggested by the evidence of wills and probate valuations. These fail to support the hypothesis that post-Famine parents lavished most of their assets on a single favoured son. Moreover, the traditional prototype of pre-Famine inter-generational transfer as egalitarian subdivision, implicit in Connell, is also oversimplified. Even before the Famine, better-off farmers sought to pass the land on to one heir, while catering for other siblings through a combination of education and direct financial assistance. After the Famine, however, the outlet of emigration and greater wealth allowed more farmers both to keep the family farm intact and to look after everybody. The Famine thus may not have changed inner parental feelings towards kin, but simply expanded the opportunities available to those parents surviving it (Ó Gráda, 1988, *ch. 5*).

The Famine has also been blamed, unjustly, for the decline of the Irish language. In fact Irish was already in rapid retreat before 1845, and less than one-third of those growing up on the eve of the Famine could speak it, compared to over two-fifths of the previous generation (Fitzgerald, 1987). Nevertheless, the Famine played its part. In aggregate terms the number of Irish-speakers alive in 1845, somewhat over 3 million in Ireland and perhaps another 0.5 million elsewhere, was the highest ever. But those who perished or emigrated were disproportionately Irish-speaking, and by 1851 the number of Irish speakers left in Ireland had fallen below 2 million[68]. Neither O'Connellite nor Fenian brands of nationalism did anything to foster Irish, and by the time a more advanced nationalist ideology adopted the old tongue it was too late.

Finally, the changes described above left their mark on Anglo-Irish literature. The sexually uninhibited and carefree images of pre-Famine Irish rural life painted by William Carleton in *Traits and Stories of the Irish Peasantry* (1830–8) or the young Anthony Trollope in *The Kellys and the O'Kellys* (published in 1847 but written earlier) faded into bleakness on every page of Carleton's *The Black Prophet* (1847) and Trollope's *Castle Richmond* (1860). Later, populist interpretations of the Famine were to provide inspiration for novelist Liam O'Flaherty, and lyric poets Seamus Heaney and Patrick Kavanagh. The Famine cameos in Canon Sheehan's *Glenanaar* (1905) and Peadar Ó Laoghaire's *Mo Scéal Féin (My Story)* (1915) – part folk memory, part autobiography – are as familiar in Ireland as, say, *Lark Rise* or *Little Dorrit* in England. Taken out of context, these often dramatic and sentimental accounts over-simplify the tragedy: yet they capture well what the camera came just too late to do.

---

[68] The 1851 census returned only 1,524,286 Irish-speakers, but many seem to have ignored the question on language proficiency.

4
Conclusion

Most traditional historiography, whether Malthusian or nationalist, implies that the Great Famine was part of Ireland's destiny. There is room, however, for an alternative view: that, taking fuller account of developments both in the domestic economy and further afield, in the end the Irish were desperately unlucky. Far from being inevitable, the series of massive and lasting fungus-induced crop failures that produced the Great Famine was utterly unpredictable. In the decades before 1845 the country had been learning how to cope with serious crop failures, not without hardship, though without massive excess mortality. But nothing quite as horrific as *Phytophthera infestans* had appeared before, in Ireland or anywhere else. Moreover, had the fungus arrived either some decades earlier or later, the damage inflicted would not have been so horrific. Earlier, reliance on the 'accursed potato' would have been less, the pressure on resources less, and governments (like that of 1822) less constrained by ideological scruples.

A postponed visitation would also have imposed less of a threat. A delay of four decades, and *Phytophthera* would have faced both Alexis Millardet's bluestone counter-remedy and a countryside more thinly peopled. Even by the 1860s the rising demand for labour in Britain and in the United States would have already absorbed hundreds of thousands of those most at risk, and thus population would have passed its peak. Government, too, would have been both better endowed and more generous. In sum the Great Famine of the 1840s, instead of being inevitable and inherent in the potato economy, was a tragic ecological accident. Ireland's experience during these years supports neither the complacency exemplified by the Whig view of political economy nor the genocide theories formerly espoused by a few nationalist historians.

Select bibliography

The works included here are listed in the text by author's name and date of publication. Donnelly (1973) and Mokyr (1985) contain more extensive bibliographies of nineteenth-century Irish economic history. Woodham-Smith's enduring but uneven *Great Hunger* (1962) remains the most comprehensive introduction to the Great Famine. Daly (1986) is short on 'emotive' description and much sounder on the economic context, while Kee (1981) provides a short sympathetic summary. The footnotes contain further references for the eager student.

Key

EHR, 2nd series	*Economic History Review*
IESH	*Irish Economic and Social History*
JEH	*Journal of Economic History*
EJ	*Economic Journal*
IHS	*Irish Historical Studies*

Almquist, E. (1979) 'Pre-Famine Ireland and the Theory of European Proto-industrialization: Evidence from the 1841 Census', *JEH* XXXIX.

Ambirajan, S. (1978) *Classical Political Economy and British Policy in India* (Cambridge). Much of ch. 3 on 'Economic Ideas and Famine Policy' could have been written about Ireland in the 1840s.

Arensberg, C. and Kimball, S. (1965) *Family and Community in Ireland* (2nd edn). World classic of rural sociology; vivid, rosy view of post-Famine society.

Black, R. D. C. (1960) *Classical Economic Thought and the Irish Question 1817–70* (Cambridge). Little on an issue where economists' dogmas were most mischievous. More indulgent than (Ambirajan, 1978).

Bourke, P. M. A. (1962) 'The Scientific Investigation of the Potato Blight in 1845–6', *IHS*, 13. This and (Bourke, 1964) are the classic accounts of the arrival of the potato blight.

Bourke, P. M. A. (1964) 'Emergence of Potato Blight', *Nature*, 22 August.

Bourke, P. M. A. (1976) 'The Irish Grain Trade, 1840–50', *IHS*, xx. Puts the claims about massive food exports during the Famine in perspective.

Bourke, P. M. A. (1965) 'The Agricultural Statistics of the 1841 Census of Ireland: A Critical Review', *EHR*, 18. Influential revision.

Bourke, P. M. A. (1968) 'The Use of the Potato Crop in Pre-Famine Ireland', *Journal of the Statistical and Social Inquiry Society of Ireland*, 12 (6), 72–96. Though the implied acreage under potatoes is too high (see Mokyr, 1981), this paper explains better than any other the lynchpin role of the potato.

Boyle, P. P. and Ó Gráda, C. (1986) 'Fertility Trends, Excess Mortality, and the Great Irish Famine', *Demography*, 23, 542–62. Estimates excess famine mortality by age and sex.

Carney, F. J. (1977) 'Aspects of pre-Famine Irish household size: Composition and Differentials', in L. M. Cullen and T. C. Smout (eds), *Comparative Aspects of Scottish and Irish Economic and Social History* (Edinburgh), pp. 32–46.

Clarkson, L. A. and Crawford, E. M. (1988) 'Dietary Directions: A Topographical Survey of Irish Diet, 1836', in R. Mitchison and P. Roebuck (eds), *Economy and Society in Scotland and Ireland 1500–1939* (Edinburgh), pp. 171–92. Highlights the quality of the potato diet.

Cousens, S. H. (1963) 'The Regional Variation in Mortality During the Great Irish Famine', *Proceedings of the Royal Irish Academy* Section C, 63, 127–49. Pioneering work, superseded in part by (Boyle and Ó Gráda, 1986) and (Mokyr, 1980b).

Cousens, S. H. (1965) 'The Regional Variation in Emigration From Ireland Between 1821 and 1841', *Institute of British Geographers, Transactions* no. 37, 15–30.

Connell, K. H. (1950) *The Population of Ireland 1750–1845* (Oxford). The true beginning of modern Irish economic history.

Connell, K. H. (1968) *Irish Peasant Society* (Oxford). Chs 1 and 2 give Connell's line on the social consequences of the Famine.

Connolly, S. (1985) *Religion and Society in Nineteenth-century Ireland* (Dublin).

Crawford, E. M. (1981) 'Indian Meal and Pellagra in Nineteenth-Century Ireland', in (Goldstrom and Clarkson). Here and in (Clarkson and Crawford, 1988) the quality of normal diet before 1845 is highlighted.

Crawford, E. M. (1984) 'Dearth, Diet, and Disease in Ireland, 1850: A Case Study of Nutritional Deficiency', *Medical History*, 28.

Crawford, E. M. (ed.) (1989) *Famine: The Irish Experience 900–1900: Subsistence Crises and Famine in Ireland* (Edinburgh). Proceedings of a conference on Irish famines held in Belfast, April 1987.

Crotty, R. D. (1966) *Irish Agricultural Production* (Cork). Cogently over-argues the case for pre-Famine adjustment.

Cullen, L. M. (1981) *The Emergence of Modern Ireland 1600–1900* (London).

Cullen, L. M. (1968) 'Irish History Without the Potato', *Past and Present*, no. 40, 72–83. Partly tongue-in-cheek title.

Daly, M. (1986) *The Great Famine in Ireland* (Dublin). Wide-ranging, useful introduction to subject.

Daultrey, S. G., Dickson, D. and Ó Gráda, C. (1981) 'Eighteenth Century Irish Population: New Perspectives from Old Sources', *JEH*, XLII (3).

Dickson, D. (1989) 'The Gap in Famines 1745–1815: A Helpful Myth?', in (Crawford).

Donnelly, J. S. (1973) *The Land and People of Nineteenth-century Cork* (London). Ch. 2 deals with the Famine.

Donnelly, J. S. (1976) 'The Irish Agricultural Depression of 1859–64', *IESH*, 3, 33–54.

Donnelly, J. S. (1989) 'The Great Famine', in W. E. Vaughan *et al.* (eds), *The New History of Ireland*, vol. 5 (Oxford).

Drake, M. (1963) 'Marriage and Population Growth in Ireland 1750–1845', *EHR*, 16, 301–17. First to draw attention to delayed marriage on the eve of the Famine.

Drake, M. (1968) 'The Irish Demographic Crisis of 1740–1', in T. W. Moody (ed.), *Historical Studies*, VI (London).

Dwyer Jr., G. P. and Lindsay, C. M. (1984) 'Robert Giffen and the Irish Potato', *American Economic Review*, 74, 188–92.

Edwards, R. D. and Williams, T. D. (eds) (1956) *The Great Famine: Studies in Irish History* (Dublin). Contains several classic studies; those by McArthur, MacDonagh, McHugh, and Thomas O'Neill are referred to in the text. But this remains an unbalanced and uneven introduction to the topic.

Fitzgerald, G. (1984) 'Estimates for Baronies of Minimum Level of Irish-speaking Amongst Successive Decennial Cohorts: 1771–1781 to 1861–1871', *Proceedings of the Royal Irish Academy*, Section C, Vol. 84, No. 3.

Fitzpatrick, D. (1984) *Irish Emigration 1801–1921* (Dublin).

Gash, Norman (1972) *Sir Robert Peel: The Life of Sir Robert Peel After 1830* (London).

Gibbon, P. (1975) 'Colonialism and the Great Starvation in Ireland 1845–9', *Race and Class*, 17. Passionate antidote to (M. Daly, 1986) and (Edwards & Williams, 1956).

Griffiths, A. R. G. (1970) 'The Irish Board of Works in the Famine Years', *Historical Journal*, XIII (4).

Grigg, D. B. (1980) *Population Growth and Agrarian Change: An Historical Perspective* (London). Ch. 10 treats Ireland as an example of 'Malthus Justified'; an interesting contrast to (Mokyr, 1983), both in its methods and findings.

Goldstrom, J. M., 'Irish Agriculture and the Great Famine', in Goldstrom and Clarkson.

Goldstrom, J. M. and Clarkson, L. A. (eds) (1981) *Population, Economy and Society* (Oxford).

Hart, J. (1960) 'Sir Charles Trevelyan at the Treasury', *English Historical Review*, LXXV. Unflattering account, based on Trevelyan's papers.

Hoffman, E. and Mokyr, J. (1983) 'Peasants, Potatoes and Poverty: Transactions Costs in Prefamine Ireland', in G. Saxonhouse and G. Wright (eds), *Technique, Spirit and Form in the Making of the Modern Economy: Essays in Honor of William N. Parker* (Greenwich, Conn.).

Hoppen, K. T. (1984) *Elections, Politics and Society in Ireland, 1832–1885* (Oxford).

Irish University Press (1968) 'Famine Series' (Shannon). An eight-volume selection of the most important Blue Books dealing with famine relief policy.

Kee, R. (1981) *Ireland: A History* (London). Kee's chapter on the Famine (pp. 77–101) is in the spirit of (Woodham-Smith, 1962).

Kennedy, L. (1983) 'Studies in Irish Econometric History', *IHS*, XXIII.

Kennedy, L. and Ollerenshaw, P. (eds) (1985) *An Economic History of Ulster 1820–1939* (Manchester).

Large, E. C. (1940) *The Advance of the Fungi* (London). Ch. 1 deals with *Phytophthera infestans*.

Larkin, E. (1972) 'The Devotional Revolution in Ireland 1850–1875', *American Historical Review*, 77. Highlights the Famine's influence on Irish religiosity.

Lee, J. (1973) *The Modernisation of Irish Society 1848–1918* (Dublin).

Lee, J. (1981) 'On the Accuracy of the Pre-famine Irish Censuses' in (Goldstrom and Clarkson, 1981).

Lynch, P. and Vaizey, J. (1960) *Guinness's Brewery in the Irish Economy 1759–1876* (Cambridge). Stimulating but a wrong-headed application of a dual economy framework to the Irish economy.

MacDonagh, O. (1956) 'Irish Emigration to the United States of America and the British Colonies During the Famine', in (Edwards and Williams).

McDonagh, O. (1961) *A Pattern of Government Growth: The Passenger Acts and Their Enforcement 1800–1860* (London).

McGregor, P. (1984) 'The Impact of the Blight Upon the Pre-Famine Rural Economy of Ireland', *Economic and Social Review*, 15.

Miller, K. (1985) *Emigrants and Exiles* (New York).

Mokyr, J. (1980a) 'Industrialization and Poverty in Ireland and the Netherlands: Some Notes towards a Comparative Case-Study', *Journal of Interdisciplinary History*, 10.

Mokyr, J. (1980b) 'The Deadly Fungus: An Econometric Investigation into the Short-term Demographic Impact of the Irish Famine, 1846–1851', *Research in Population Economics*, 2.

Mokyr, J. (1981) 'Irish History with the Potato', *IESH*, 8.

Mokyr, J. (1983) *Why Ireland Starved: A Quantitative and Analytical History of the Irish Economy, 1800–1845* (first edn, London; revised edn, 1985). Vigorous, brilliant, much-discussed.

Mokyr, J. and Ó Gráda, C. (1982) 'Emigration and Poverty in Prefamine Ireland', *Explorations in Economic History*, 19.

Mokyr, J. and Ó Gráda, C. (1984) 'New Developments in Irish Population History, 1700–1845', *EHR*, 47. Outlines progress since Connell (1950).

O'Brien, G. (1985) 'Workhouse Management in Pre-famine Ireland', *Proceedings of the Royal Irish Academy* 86, Section C, 113–34.

O'Farrell, P. (1976) 'Emigrant Attitudes and Behaviour as a Source for Irish History', *Historical Studies*, x.

Ó Gráda, C. (1984) 'Malthus and the Pre-Famine Economy', in A. Murphy (ed.), *Economists and the Irish Economy* (Dublin).

Ó Gráda, C. (1988) *Ireland Before and After the Famine: Explorations in Economic History 1800–1930* (Manchester).

O'Neill, K. (1984) *Family and Farm in Pre-famine Ireland: The Parish of Killashandra* (Madison).

O'Neill, T. (1989) 'The Food Crisis of the 1890s', in (Crawford).

O'Rourke, J. (1902) *History of the Great Irish Famine of 1847*, 3rd edn (Dublin).

Ó Tuathaigh, G. (1972) *Ireland Before the Famine 1798–1848* (Dublin).

Post, J. (1977) *The Last Great Subsistence Crisis in the Western World* (Baltimore). Useful book, but the subject matter is neither Ireland's (1846–50) nor Finland's (1867–8) Great Famines but the more diffuse crisis striking much of Europe in 1817–19.

Post, J. (1985) *Food Shortage, Climatic Variability and Epidemic Disease in Preindustrial Europe: The Mortality Peak in the Early 1740s* (Ithaca).

Royle, S. A. (1984) 'Irish Famine Relief in the Early Nineteenth Century', *IESH*, xi.

Salaman, R. N. (1985) *The History and Social Influence of the Potato* (new edn, Cambridge). Though dated, Chs 11–18 have an interesting account of the potato and Ireland. Compare (Cullen, 1968).

Sen, A. (1981) *Poverty and Famines* (Oxford).

Senior, N. W. (1868) *Essays, Conversations and Journals Relating to Ireland* (London). Work, some of it influential, by an economist whose contempt for the Irish bordered on the racist.

Solar, P. M. (1984) 'Why Ireland Starved: A Critical Review of the Econometric Results', *IESH*, XI.

Solar, P. M. (1987) 'The Singularity of the Great Famine', in (Crawford). Based on a statistical analysis of pre-1845 crop yields.

Trevelyan, C. (1847) *The Irish Crisis* (London).

Walford, C. (1878) 'The Famines of the World, Past and Present', *Journal of the Royal Statistical Society*, vol. 41, 433–526, and vol. 42 (1879), 79–265. Idiosyncratic though still useful survey.

Watkins, S. C. and Menken, J. (1985) 'Famines in Historical Perspective', *Population and Development Review*, 11. Questions the effectiveness of famines as Malthusian positive checks.

Woodham-Smith, C. (1962) *The Great Hunger: Ireland, 1845–59* (London). Uneven and much maligned by Irish historians; still the best narrative account of the Famine's horrors, however.

Woods, C. (1987) 'American Travellers in Ireland Before and During the Great Famine: A Case of Culture-Shock', in Wolfgang Zach and Heinz Kosok (eds), *Literary Interrelations: Ireland, England and the New World* (Tübingen).

Bibliographical update and commentary

A decade ago, the Great Irish Famine remained a neglected research topic. For reasons explained above (pp. 2–3), Irish historians tended to shy away from it. That has changed a good deal in the past few years, and the Famine's sesquicentennial will doubtless generate many more conference papers and monographs. On the whole, recent research rejects the sanitized and quasi-apologetic stance that marked some earlier work. It has filled some important gaps in the economic, political, and cultural history of the Famine. It still remains for historians to attempt a more comparative approach to the tragedy – to assess the Irish experience against famines elsewhere, both in the 1840s and since. Further 'micro' research into all aspects of the Famine (and not just the administration of relief!) in different regions in Ireland should also reap dividends.

Bourke, Austin (1993) *The Visitation of God? The Potato and the Irish Famine*, Dublin: Lilliput Press. A selection of Bourke's published and unpublished work; contains useful bibliography.

Grant, James (1990) 'The Great Famine and the poor law in the province of Ulster: the rate-in-aid issue of 1849', *Irish Historical Studies*, vol. 27, 30–47.

Gray, Peter (1993) 'Punch and the Great Famine', *History Ireland*, 1(2), 26–33.

Gray, Peter (1994) 'Potatoes and providence: British government's responses to the Great Famine', *Bullán*, 1(1), 75–90. Study of the ideological constraints on government action.

Hatton, T. J. and Williamson, J. G. (1993) 'After the famine: emigration from Ireland 1850–1913', *Journal of Economic History*, vol. 54(3), 575–600.

Kerr, Donal A. (1994) *'A Nation of Beggars'? Priests, People, and Politics in Famine Ireland, 1846–1852*, Oxford: Oxford University Press.

Kinealy, Christine (1994) *This Great Calamity: the Irish Famine 1845–52*, Dublin: Gill & Macmillan. Strong on the administrative side.

Lindsay, Deirdre and Fitzpatrick, David (1993) *Records of the Irish Famine: A Guide to Local Archives, 1840–1855*, Dublin: Irish Famine Network. A survey of parish registers and poor law records.

McGregor, Patrick (1989) 'Demographic pressure and the Irish famine: Malthus after Mokyr', *Land Economics*, vol. 65, 228–38. For Malthus, against Mokyr.

Morash, Chris (1989) *The Hungry Voice: The Poetry of the Irish Famine*, Dublin: Irish Academic Press.

O Gráda, Cormac (1992) 'Making history in Ireland in the 1940s and 1950s: The Saga of *The Great Famine*', *The Irish Review*, No. 12. An account of how Edwards and Williams (1956) was written.

O'Rourke, Kevin (1991) 'Did the Great Famine matter?', *Journal of Economic History*, vol. 51(1), 1–22. Sophisticated counterfactual analysis.

Vincent, Joan (1992) 'A Political Orchestration of the Irish Famine: County Fermanagh, May 1847', in Marilyn Silverman and P. H. Gulliver (eds), *Approaching the Past: Historical Anthropology through Irish Case Studies*, New York: Columbia University Press, 75–98.

Glossary

Age-cohort depletion: the proportion of some base-year age group, say those aged 10–19, 'missing' in a later census, e.g. those aged 20–29 ten years later. This measure has been used by Irish historians (e.g. Fitzpatrick, 1984) as a check on (or substitute) for emigration statistics.

Boserupian: refers to thesis advanced by Danish economist Ester Boserup that population change typically forces land-saving technical change, or the application of techniques previously in cold storage, in agriculture. In this view, to paraphrase Malthus, population growth leads not to misery but to energy.

Efficiency wage: if the productivity of workers is enhanced by wage payments above the equilibrium market-clearing wage, it may repay employers to pay them an 'efficiency wage'.

Entitlements: according to Indian economist Amartya Sen, famines often (and typically in this century) are not the product of food short-falls, but of the inability of the poor to command the food available, through their labour or the product of their labour. The poor's 'entitlements' to food cannot prevent them from starving.

External economies: the definition of Alfred Marshall, who suggested the concept, can hardly be bettered: 'savings dependent on the general development of industry [which] can often be secured by the concentration of many small businesses of a similar character in particular localities'.

Giffen good: a good the demand for which rises with a rise in price. For most economists, such goods are like the Loch Ness Monster, occasionally reported, never observed.

Pareto optimum: an allocation of resources (e.g. food) is Pareto-efficient if no other allocation can improve the lot of one person or group without making somebody else worse off.

Poverty trap: an economy, group, or individual finds itself in a 'poverty trap' if it cannot, through poverty, respond to incentives that would better its condition.

Skewed: the frequency distributions of many phenomena, such as annual grain yields, or adult heights, or tosses of a coin, have a regular, bell-shaped form. Many others are skewed either to the right or left; for example, since marriages above the modal age are far more spread out than those below the mode, the frequency distribution of marriage age is said to be skewed to the right. When a distribution is moderately skewed, we have:

$$Mean - \text{Mode} = 3(Mean - Median)$$

Whence the claim in the text.

Terms of trade: the ratio of a country's export prices to its import prices.

Index

New Studies in Economic and Social History

Titles in the series available from Cambridge University Press:

Previously published as

Studies in Economic History

Titles in the series available from the Macmillan Press Limited

12. H. McLeod
Religion and the working classes in nineteenth-century Britain

13. J.D. Marshall
The Old Poor Law 1795–1834: second edition

14. R.J. Morris
Class and class consciousness in the industrial revolution, 1750–1850

15. P.K. O'Brien
The economic effects of the American civil war

16. P.L. Payne
British entrepreneurship in the nineteenth century

17. G.C. Peden
Keynes, the treasury and British economic policy

18. M.E. Rose
The relief of poverty, 1834–1914

19. J. Thirsk
England's agricultural regions and agrarian history, 1500–1750

20. J.R. Ward
Poverty and progress in the Caribbean, 1800–1960

Economic History Society

The Economic History Society, which numbers around 3,000 members, publishes the *Economic History Review* four times a year (free to members) and holds an annual conference.

Enquiries about membership should be addressed to

The Assistant Secretary
Economic History Society
PO Box 70
Kingswood
Bristol
BS15 5TB

Full-time students may join at special rates.